A FLAVOUR OF FRANCE

For Prue, with
thanks for many
kindnesses.
If Odette
would have
signed this, she
would probably
have said,
"Bon Appetit
and happy reading."
Tony.
October 1999.

A
FLAVOUR
OF FRANCE

Odette Murray

wood engravings by Jonathan Gibbs

CANONGATE

First published in 1988 by
Canongate Publishing Limited
17 Jeffrey Street, Edinburgh, Scotland

Text © 1988 Odette Murray
Wood engravings © 1988 Jonathan Gibbs

British Library Cataloguing in Publication Data
Murray. Odette
A flavour of France.
1. Food : French dishes
I. Title
641.3′00944
ISBN 0-86241-166-1

Typeset in 11pt Imprint
by BAS, Over Wallop, Hampshire
Printed by Billings and Son Ltd, Worcester

INGREDIENTS

to my mother
from whom I learnt so much

ACKNOWLEDGEMENTS

This book would never have been possible without the help of many friends: Valerie Humphries, Maud Crawford, Flick Farquhar and Mary Christic. Mary was asked to type only a few pages and was still hard at work many drafts and several weeks later.

A special thankyou also to my editor at Canongate who encouraged me from beginning to end and to my husband Tony for his practical help and constant support.

I have drawn inspiration and some quotations from Henri Castellot's *Histoire à Table* and the *Larousse Gastronomique* 1938.

INTRODUCTION

In the early sixties, I left the south of France to marry a Scot and live in rural Scotland. The lingering accents of the Auld Alliance were loud enough to stir me into thinking that, readily and easily, I could be turned into a true Scot, body and soul. But as far as the body goes, mine was soon craving for French cuisine as I had known it in the south. To me it was much more than just eating: it was a whole way of life.

When getting married, the romantic but cautious French sign a legal document, a marriage agreement, *contrat de mariage*. For a French woman in exile, trips to France were the only demand. This appealed much to my husband. I wanted to keep in touch with my roots, my friends, a way of life where the sun is all important and all powerful. Cyrano de Bergerac, a Gascon like d'Artagnan, with much panache and wit, won fame for Rostand, his spiritual father. In 'Chantecler', one of his lesser known plays, he, the writer, dedicated a hymn to the sun, 'O toi, soleil, without which nothing would be like what it is...' a title and a theme that fascinated me as a young teenager; the worship for the Sun God seemed very natural. The young woman who married in a beautiful northern country, felt often that the sun had gone somewhere else and deserted the place.

Eventually I realised that I was bringing the sunshine into my cooking. A vital part of me was alive and well. Naturally the first recipes were the ones I had enjoyed in my native *Sud-Ouest*. As visits to the south and other parts of my country multiplied, I became keener and more knowledgeable about food and cooking. Subsequent visits to other parts of Europe further developed my curiosity in this field—the similarities and differences intrigued and stimulated me. Over the years I have become a convinced citizen of Europe, especially in my kitchen!

It would take too long to go back to those early days in my Scottish home and the frustrations attached to everyday cooking. What was provided at the table, the monotonous repetitions, did little to lift the morale. Neither typical nor representative maybe, but unfortunately, my first taste of Scotland. The elderly Scottish cook would not suffer interference.

The thought of an invasion of frogs' legs and slimy snails may have strengthened her resolution.

Twenty five years ago the Scottish larder and Scottish cuisine suffered from a scarcity of goods. There was great use of artificial flavourings, additives or substitutes—a legacy of the war restrictions perhaps. In my moments of despair, Gallic exaggeration takes over, and it seemed, at times, that the dark ages of cooking were upon me, with only malt vinegar and coffee extract, salad cream and no oil—as for *olive* oil, it was eventually tracked down in the chemist's shop! A small bottle with no sunshine left in it. The list was long then. Now the choice and variety have improved remarkably, and with some determination one can find almost anything, even discover other things that one did not know about.

My practical experience was not extensive, but my head was full of memories centred upon my mother's kitchen and the infinite variety of its tastes and smells. There the activities followed, and punctuated, the rhythm of the seasons. For a child, it was a fabulous calendar. The real year started with the first cherries, picked while the cuckoo teased us from some far away tree. Strawberries and early peaches soon followed; an irresistable combination with red or white wine, especially if wild strawberries were added. On Sundays there were always welcoming and inviting smells drifting out of the kitchen. My mouth waters at the thought of the first spring chicken, roasting slowly—filled with green olives, garlic and chunks of *saucisse de Toulouse*, highly seasoned and full of flavour. These sausages were quite a contrast to the ones I found here twenty years ago—and so I started making my own. My first attempt at *charcuterie* was not an outright success; the filling was easy, but the packaging frustrating. Nowadays my obliging butcher takes on that side of the operation.

In late summer, the juices of the chicken were sharpened with
verjus (squeezed, unripe sour grapes). Nowadays. I use lemon or lime instead. A little later in the year came the tasting of the new wine, fresh and tingling, pleasant, but without the promise of a great future. The days were shorter and friends would come along in the evening. The first roast chestnuts were enjoyed with *le vin nouveau*, and stories were told into the night. Imagination
is lively in this part of France, where Gascony and Languedoc

meet.

In my corner of provincial France, originality and versatility are not essential for everyday cooking. Tradition is rich and varied, the need for change is minimal. Had I lived there, I would probably have followed the established way. In Scotland I faced a new reality, a stimulating challenge. It meant experimenting, improvising and adapting, to live pleasurably.

For the British cook, everyday cooking is much more of an effort than it is for the French. To start with, the budget allocated to food is usually smaller. If inspiration or energy fails, when time is at a premium, there are no *charcuteries*, *pâtisseries* or *crèmeries* to rush to , especially in the rural areas. Worst of all, to me, is the absence of markets, like the ones found everywhere in France, from Normandy to Provence. I still miss them. Suddenly there is a pang, an urge to wander through those lost paradises. Yet in spite of all the difficulties early on, I have been pleasantly surprised by the originality, the versatility, the knowledge and the *esprit d'aventure* of some of my friends in Britain. In the last twenty years, there have been so many changes for the better, that everyday cooking has become easier, more appealing and more fun. Delicatessens and supermarkets of one kind or another are largely responsible for this.

Suffering from a certain native restlessness, I try to keep monotony and boredom at bay. It is perhaps the reason for my special interest in everyday cooking. I like to think that, out of the melting pot, my cooking has emerged with a difference— originally French—traditional with a Mediterranean accent, now revised and adapted after twenty or so years of life in a country with a Northern climate and different traditions. It is simply *cuisine de tous les jours* influenced by supplies from the shops, from my little vegetable garden and, with luck, from what my friends can spare from theirs.

The woods where we live provide us with game and mushrooms, mainly chanterelles and a few boletus or *cèpes*, as they are called in France. It is a great thrill for a French native in Scotland; the picking is quiet and leisurely, there is no need to start before dawn, before the rush of the searching crowds. Alas, there are changes in the air, threatening this happy *status quo*. Enterprising Scots have discovered the French addiction to these little orange mushrooms that travel relatively well, and 3 send them to French kitchens and restaurants, and even to Germany.

For everyday cooking, the influence of the prevailing mood is an important catalyst. On gloomy days, when there is a mood of despondency in the air and cooking has no great appeal, specialities brought back from France offer me instant gastronomy and instant flashback. There are pâtés and varied regional charcuteries, like stuffed goose necks; spicy fish soup, bottled asparagus, artichokes, quince and apricots in syrup; jams, home-made from peaches, cherries, figs—with extra flavour given by freshly picked fruit, ripened on the tree. Occasionally on the shelf can be found one or two tins of *foie gras*—the gifts of generous friends who think that Christmas would not be possible without it. They do wonders for the morale, at any time of the year, with a glass of wine and good company, of course.

A few years ago in France our son, then seventeen, was given an introduction to celebration meals and traditional gastronomy: a coming of age, *à la française*. There was champagne and *foie gras* on three successive occasions—rather taxing for anybody. Unimpressed at the end of the festivities, he whispered, 'That thing, foie gras, is overrated'. No mention of the champagne! I presume a surfeit of *foie gras* will not occur often. Personally, I do appreciate *that thing*, but I suspect the pleasure is inseparable from my happy memories and joyous occassions *en famille*, or with friends.

Overall, I like *cuisine allégée*, lighter cooking, whether or not traditional. It is neither a diet, nor a plan of austerity—mainly a matter of taste and a feeling of well-being. Enjoy today without painful regrets tomorrow.

I was brought up in that part of France where traditionally one tends to cook with oil rather than butter. The early Mediterranean influence lives on. Even in specific recipes where tradition requires cooking with butter, especially frying, I try to compromise and use part oil and part butter, without losing the flavour of the butter. Not being a pastry cook by inclination,
for everyday meals I make a quick (and good) shortcrust pastry using oil. It is ideal for *quiches* and all their variations.

Recently I baked a *tarte aux prunes*—an open fruit pie with greengages (*reines-claudes*)—using olive oil for the pastry. It was surprisingly good and crisp, the fruitiness of the oil just noticeable, and very pleasant. Pears were tried the next time, adding a taste of honey to the fruit—no innovation, simply the same combination of oil and honey which ancient Greeks used for their pastries.

As I was settling into my kitchen (the cook eventually left!) and cooking my own way, questions came up occasionally that could not be ignored. What about garlic? Do they, or do they not, approve of it in Scotland? Would they tolerate it just a tiny bit? I am no garlic fiend, but being a southerner, its flavour and aroma could not be forsaken altogether. On the other hand, I had no wish to be ostracised. An old Scottish book on vegetable growing, written by a minister, gave me the answer, in no uncertain terms: *Not designed for food to man in a state of society, and hermits, if they choose, may find enough of it growing wild in woods and glens which they naturally frequent.* In Rome, do as the Romans do; a sound principle, maybe, but not in my kitchen!

Nevertheless, the issue had to be handled with care. This is equally true in France where opinions and tastes are divided and range from intense dislike to immoderate and inconsiderate liking. One evening with Scottish friends in Britain, I was given and tried for the first time, bread with garlic butter. I was surprised and delighted at the combination. Garlic bread as it was eaten in my rural south was very different: simple and unsophisticated—a clove of garlic rubbed vigourously over crisp and crusty bread, with olive oil trickled over it and a sprinkling of sea salt. A fiery and pungent mixture indeed; *paleolithic* cooking it is called sometimes. In the right environment it is very good, especially with a bunch of sweet grapes. *Chapons* are mini-versions—garlicky croûtons mixed with a crisp salad of endives, *chicorée*, preferably the curly type, known in the markets as *la frisée*. With the first tasting of bread and garlic butter, I realised that afficionados thrived on both sides of the Channel.

A few years ago, during an autumn holiday, we stopped in a farm of Lomagne to buy our winter provision of garlic. The farmer's wife was chatty and keen to know more about *l'Angleterre*. I was eager to have her reaction to garlic bread made in Britain. I explained the recipe—the garlic butter, the baguette, the wrapping in foil, and the hot, tasty crunching. She looked at me in admiration, or was it concern? 'Oh Madame, you do like things to be strong!' she said, in her uninhibited southern accent.

Everyday cooking is, on the whole, seasonal; every month brings a renewal of interest and recipes. November, for instance, is the time to buy two, maybe three, pumpkins. They keep a long time. In my youth, they were turned into soup I cared little for; lantern making was more exciting—to lighten the night and frighten the witches. Toasting the seeds was left to the children, nothing was wasted. Piled high at the side of the road, their large sizes, mixed shapes, and bright colourings brought a touch of magic to the autumn countryside. Giants of one hundred pounds and more are not unusual. What a *pièce*

de résistance for a garden show! The *citrouille* of Cinderella fame is large, pale in colour and poor in flavour, while the *potiron* is more striking in appearance, showy inside and out.

Most of this century the British have not been renowned for their cooking. Happily this is fast changing. In *A Book About Paris* (1922), George and Pearl Adam wrote, *An Englishman remains a barbarian in French ideas in his habit of looking upon food as a necessity rather than a pleasure, and that necessity a nuisance!* Whenever or wherever this happens it is sad, and I look upon a lack of interest in food almost as a handicap or a lack of *joie de vivre*. Who would choose willingly to turn a vital daily necessity into a boring routine? It does not mean that food must be fancy, expensive or sophisticated to be enjoyed. It is true that conviviality is important around the table, but even on one's own a pleasant meal should be enjoyed. It lifts the body and the mind. You owe it to yourself!

In this book some chapters are built around one recipe with variations and adaptations. Their excellence has been established for years and they encapsulate my idea of French cooking as I see it, from a distance. The great diversity from one end of the country to the other is amazing and is influenced by the climate, the local riches, or by mixing and borrowing from neighbouring countries. This is why, in between my main recipes, there are other simple easy recipes which I felt would do well in Britain and would give a wider choice. Nonetheless this is only a small selection to give the reader a taste—just some

6 of the flavours of France.

Potages

POTAGES POUR TOUS
Soups

A few decades ago soup was an essential part of people's diet in the countryside, while bread was the staple food. Vegetables, meat and fish were cooked in varying quantities according to the budget, the time of year or the area. Soup became one of the most nutritious, filling and economical of dishes.

Good hearty soups are usually popular with men, especially on cold days. In Ste Hélène, Napoleon occasionally asked for a simple soldiers' soup 'where the spoon stood to attention', *au garde à vous*—nostalgia perhaps for soldiers' brotherhood, or simply the fact that on Ste Hélène Napoleon had a large appetite, as Sir Walter Scott tells us in his biography of Bonaparte. 'He preferred plain food and ate plentifully and with an apparent appetite'.

As a young child with a bird's appetite and fussy with it , good substantial soup was not my favourite part of the meal. Chicken or beef consommé, and puréed vegetable soup, were better and easier to eat. Parents remained firm in the face of this resistance. Everywhere, in every family, it was the same tune—'Eat your soup if you want to grow up' or, 'If you don't eat your soup you won't grow any taller than Tante Lucie'. There were more immediate threats—'no soup, no pudding'. Occasionally my mother would appeal to my conscience—'Think of all those starving people, they would be so grateful'— but I could not see how one could help the other!

What changes since then! Soups have become more sophisticated *potages*, elegant preparations such as the one Bocuse prepared for Giscard D'Estaing: individual soup bowls with a crusty lid of puff pastry, hiding an aromatic truffle soup—not the evening potage for the average family though! But all is not lost. Soups are still *de rigueur* for the evening meal in many families. The ones mentioned here are a mixed bunch —traditional, simple, something for all tastes.

There are a few recipes for soups with southern undertones, easy to make anywhere. They can be changed slightly, simplified or made more sophisticated according to the ingredients 9

available, the occasion or the time of year. In the south west
of France there are *tourins* galore with garlic only, with garlic
and onion, with garlic and tomato, with onions and tomatoes.
The tomatoes make it more of a summer soup. Sprinkle with
finely chopped parsley (the flat variety if possible) or a little basil.
These soups are all quick to prepare and full of flavour.

TOURIN À L'AIL
Garlic Soup

In this book (and in this recipe) I occasionally mention a way
of binding a sauce as a *liaison*! Each time I mention it I do so
with circumspection since my son assures me that no one will
take seriously the word *liaison* as a term of binding!

In fact, it is a classical culinary term, often used in English
editions of such works as *Larousse Gastronomique* and,
moreover, is highly descriptive. So let us now set the record
straight!

For 4 to 5 people
1 head of garlic (or 2 for a creamier and better flavour)
3 tbsp olive oil or lard (goose fat originally)
2 small yolks
1 tbsp wine vinegar
1¼ litres/2¼ pints water
Salt and pepper
Parsley stems
Thyme
Bread, stale or dried

Peel the garlic and fry gently on all sides, cover with a lid and
cook for a few minutes without browning. Add the hot water,
thyme, parsley stems and seasoning. Boil for 20 minutes. Toast
the sliced bread, cut into bite-sized pieces to add to each plate.
The texture of continental type loaf (Italian or Polish) is possibly
the nearest to the type used in the country. Baguette type is
more likely now.

Remove the thyme and parsley, and purée the soup (using
a mixer or a *mouli-légumes*). In a small bowl, mix the yolks with
the vinegar and a little hot soup, then add gradually to the pan,

10

off the heat. This *liaison* or binding sauce, flavours, colours and thickens the *tourin*. Serve the garlic soup with the bread. Hand round a bowl of grated cheese (Gruyère, Emmenthal or Cheddar) if something more nutritious and filling is required. A few croûtons and a sprinkling of finely chopped parsley make a more sophisticated soup.

I remember my mother adding to such soups a liaison which sharpened the flavour. Did she use vinegar because free-range hens, fed on grain, supplemented their diets with tasty morsels, uncovered by enthusiastic scratching around? The hens obviously found the insects exceedingly tasty, the worms juicy; but I think it made the eggs taste stronger. Nowadays, when I make a *liaison* with yolks for a cream sauce, I add lemon juice, the flavour is lighter and in keeping with the cream.

Another version includes garlic and tomatoes (with or without onions). The tomatoes must be ripe and well flavoured. A large tin of tomatoes is excellent, and ready peeled!

CRÈME DE COURGETTE
Courgette soup

For 4 to 5 people
750 g/1½ lb young courgettes (peeled or unpeeled)
½ litre/17 fl. oz water (or light chicken stock)
¼ litre/9 fl.oz milk
4—5 portions processed cheese, made with Gruyère, or Italian
  Fontina
Salt and Pepper
Chives (optional)

If the courgettes are peeled the soup is pure white. With the peel the soup is nicely coloured and has more flavour. Cook the courgettes in the stock, then liquidise very finely, add the milk and the cheese. Cook slowly until well blended but do not boil. Season to taste. Served hot, as a creamy soup, the flavour is pleasant and rather elusive. It can also be served cold with chopped chives. This recipe was given to me by a Spanish friend, the only soup her young children would eat with pleasure.

CRÈME DE CHAMPIGNONS
Cream of Mushroom Soup

This is best made with cultivated mushrooms, mixed with dried cèpes.

For 4 to 6 people
250 g/½ lb mushrooms, sliced—the larger ones have more flavour.
A few dried mushrooms
250 g/½ lb onions
1—2 garlic cloves
1 small bunch of parsley, finely chopped
1 litre/1¾ pints light stock
1 dsp flour
1 yolk
1 dsp thick cream
Salt and pepper
2 tbsp oil, or oil and butter

If using dried mushrooms, cover with a little water and leave to soak for a couple of hours beforehand. Soften the onions and garlic in the oil. Add the ordinary mushrooms. When the onions and mushrooms are cooked, sprinkle the flour over them, and stir while it cooks for a few minutes. Slowly add the cèpes and the water in which they were infused and the stock. Cook gently for 25 to 30 minutes. Liquidise. Bring to the boil again, check the seasoning and add, off the heat, the cream and the yolk mixed together with a little soup. Just before serving sprinkle the soup with the chopped parsley.

CALDO VERDE
Portuguese Soup

I first sampled this green soup while staying in Portugal with friends. It is simple, yet different. There, they use a local cabbage which looks unusually tall, the size of an overgrown Brussel sprout plant, with long leaves growing all along the thick stem. By the end of the season their silhouette is rather gaunt, like a mini palm tree—all the lower leaves having been pulled out! In Normandy one can see similar silhouettes in garden cottages.

These are the tasty fodder for domestic pets, especially rabbits.
In Scotland, I find curly kale a good substitute. Green leaves
from spring cabbage, if tender, would be equally good and
well-flavoured.

For 4 to 6 people
½ kg/1 lb potatoes (chopped fairly fine)
300 g/10 oz curly kale or spring cabbage
1¼ litres/2¼ pints chicken stock
3 tbsp olive oil

Boil the potatoes and the stock together to make a thin smooth
soup. Liquidise then add the curly tips sliced very finely; the
quality of the soup depends on it. The easiest way is to hold
tightly the bunch of leaves in one hand and, using a sharp knife,
slice as finely as possible on a chopping board. Add to the boiling
soup and cook for 2 to 4 minutes. Take off the heat and stir
in 2 to 3 tbsp of olive oil. Check the seasoning—salt and pepper.
It is a pleasant, unsophisticated country soup. A bowl of grated
cheese can be put in the middle of the table and scattered on
the soup to make a slightly more substantial meal.

SOUPE DE MARRON
Chestnut Soup

This chestnut soup is not too lengthy to prepare. The sweetness
of the chestnuts is nicely balanced by the celery and the lemon;
the cream binds all the flavours smoothly.

For 4 to 5 people
½ kg/1 lb dry chestnuts (make sure they are not old or stale)
2 large bay leaves
1 large onion
1 carrot
3—4 celery stalks
100 ml/3 fl.oz cream, single or double
1 litre/1¾ pints light stock or water
Juice and grated rind of 1 lemon
30 g/1 oz butter
1 tbsp oil

Cover the chestnuts and bay leaves with water (twice their weight in water, approx). Cook until soft (about 30 minutes) with a lid on. This can be done ahead. Chop all the vegetables finely. Fry the onion and carrot in the oil and when soft add the chopped celery. After a few minutes add the softened and strained chestnuts. Add the stock and cook for a further 20 minutes. Sieve or liquidise the soup. Bring to the boil again and finally, off the heat, mix in the cream sharpened with the lemon juice. Check the seasoning. A little freshly ground pepper goes well.

While staying in Corsica one autumn, I was reminded that the island's diet was once based on chestnuts (as in the Massif Central). The tree was essential for survival and called *l'arbre à pain*—the bread tree! The season started with fresh chestnuts followed by chestnut flour. Dried chestnuts came last. If the storage went wrong, insects or mould were quick to take over and damage the supply immediately. Alphonse Daudet tells in *Paysage Gastronomique* how he shared with a shepherd and his

PULENDA family their meagre fare, a *pulenda*, chestnut flour mixed with water and cooked on a smoky fire. The flour was bad, and the flavour terrible. Pot luck indeed, but it was the best they could offer with cheese made from ewe's milk. Such basic winter diets, found not all that long ago in poorer areas, went unchanged for centuries.

The Corsican way of life has changed beyond recognition in the last few decades. When the chestnut season is in full swing and the first chestnut flour comes out of the mills, the islanders celebrate and meet to eat the *pulenda*. Once we were asked to join in the festivities. As an outsider I felt it was something of a ritual, in memory of the olden days, the forefathers, the Corsican spirit. Their celebrations reminded me of the celebrations of the Scots with the haggis on Burns' night. The Corsican *pulenda* was served with traditional specialities, well flavoured

FIGATELLI *figatelli* (liver sausage) cooked in a huge fireplace. Eggs were fried in the sausage fat, for better flavour but not digestibility.

BROCCIU There was delicately flavoured fresh *brocciu*—creamy goat cheese.

All the cooking was done by men, possibly the only day in

14 the year when they were in charge. Two men were needed to

cook the *pulenda*; soon I realised why. It was prepared in a huge pot and stirred with a *pulendagjhu*, a large version of a Scottish spurtle, used for stirring porridge. As the mixture thickened, the stirring became more and more arduous. One man held the pot while the other kept stirring the *pulenda*, more and more slowly, with both hands, amidst great hilarity. Suddenly we were summoned around the big table. The *pulenda* was ready. It was poured by the two men onto a floured cloth, more chestnut flour was sprinkled on top of this *bouillie* or gruel. The corners of the cloth were occasionally lifted while the pullenda got colder and thickened like cooling lava! With a slender bough stripped of its leaves the *pulenda* was dished most efficiently and neatly on to the plates.

The flavour is pleasant and sweet; the texture is thick and filling. It used to replace bread, until fairly recently. The experience was interesting, but the prospect of the daily diet did not appeal. I would prefer a variation with a lighter mixture, such as *nicci* (pancake made with chestnut flour, using an old- fashioned griddle) and served with creamy *brocciu*. But, if nothing else, I was assured of the versatility of chestnuts. A dry one can be sucked like a sweet—it is certainly cheaper than the melt-in-the-mouth *marron glacé*, better for the teeth and not so addictive either! For *goûter* or four o'clock break, one grandmother complained that school children had become far too demanding, 'In my days,' she said, 'we had to make do with a slice of bread sprinkled with chestnut flour, and had fun blowing it at each others faces!'

SOUPE AUX MOULES
Quick Mussel Soup

This soup is easy, quick and quite cheap to make. I discovered tinned mussels in brine years ago when I made *paellas* that reminded me of student days in Spain in the early sixties. Fresh mussels obviously have more flavour; do use them when available or when time permits.

For 4 people
1 tin mussels in brine (not vinegar)
 or ½ lb fresh mussels, well soaked, scrubbed and shelled
2 medium sized onions

2 — 3 garlic cloves
Bay leaf and a pinch of thyme
1 glass (20 cl) dry white wine
1 dsp flour
Saffron, a good pinch
2 yolks, lemon juice or 1 tbsp cream
30 g/1 oz butter and 2 spoonfuls oil
Parsley — 1 tsp finely chopped
1 litre/1¾ pints water, or *court-bouillon* if available.

Finely chop the onion and fry gently in the butter and some of the oil until soft but barely coloured. Add the flour. Stir and cook for a short while. Slowly add the wine, the saffron, the herbs and the stock. Cook for 30 minutes or so and season. The saffron not only colours the soup but flavours it in a unique way. When this is ready and well flavoured, add the mussels; they must come to the boil, and no more. Remove from the heat and add the yolks diluted with lemon juice and a little hot soup. Mix with the rest. Serve with finely chopped parsley and small croûtons fried in olive oil, flavoured with a clove of garlic or two. Make sure the garlic does not turn brown. Remove it before adding the bread.

For a change, add, when the onions are cooking, three tender celery sticks, sliced finely or medium sized, sliced fennel. These two vegetables in their own way, are excellent. It does mean though that the soup needs to cook longer in the first stage.

BOUILLABAISSE
RISOTTO
    Saffron works wonders with fish and rice. (Fish soup, *bouillabaisse*, *risotto*, to mention only one or two classics.) Added to the water when making pastry it flavours and colours it most attractively.

SOUPE À L'OIGNON GRATINÉE
French Onion Soup

This is one of the best known French soups, very simple but too often carelessly prepared.

300 g/ 10 oz onions
30 g/ 1 oz flour
30 g/ 1 oz butter
1 tbsp oil
1 litre/1¾ pints good chicken stock (or chicken cube and water)
a small glass of white wine
150—200 g/5—7 oz grated cheese (Gruyère or Emmenthal with
    a little Parmesan)
Slices of French bread (baguette type or Italian, stale or oven
    dried)
Pepper from the mill, a good sprinkling
Salt

Slice the onions finely and cook in the fat, not too briskly. When they are softening and are lightly coloured, sprinkle with the flour, stir and cook until the *roux* acquires a light caramel shade. Gradually add the stock and the wine. Cook for another 25 to 30 minutes. Add plenty of pepper but check before adding salt. Take into consideration the saltiness of the cheese and the stock. When the soup is ready, ladle it into a soup tureen or individual ovenware soup bowls. Lay a few slices of bread on the top and press gently below the surface. Sprinkle generously with the cheese. Let it colour in the oven. The top layer is thick and crusty and combines successfully with the well flavoured soup.

For a thicker and even more filling soup, lay at the bottom of the tureen a few thin slices of bread and cheese. Proceed as before and colour in the oven (around 20 to 30 minutes). The bread swells, becomes soft, almost creamy. The crusty top looks inviting, especially when returning home late at night. Once prepared, the soup can wait until the oven stage. With an automatic oven, the soup is ready when required and will wait without spoiling. Going back home on a cold night, the thought of the soup in the oven is a cheering one. The generous aroma of the *gratinée* will welcome you and revive you instantly, as it did the French *noctambules* in the Paris district of *les Halles*. They ended their night while the market people started their early day with *soupe à l'oignon*, often boosted with port.   17

VELOUTÉ DE POISSON
Simple Fish Soup

For 4 people
2 fillets whiting
1 litre/1¾ pints *court-bouillon* or fish stock
50 g/2 oz plain flour
50 g/2 oz butter
2 yolks
2 dsp cream
Juice of 1 lemon
Salt and pepper
1 tsp parsley, chopped

COURT
BOUILLON

When making a good *court-bouillon* for a large fish, keep it afterwards to make a good, economical fish soup. (Alternatively, make a good fish stock with fish heads and bones.) Boil the *court-bouillon* for a few minutes to concentrate the flavours. Meanwhile make a *roux* with the flour and butter. Dilute slowly with the fish stock, and cook for a minute or two. In a bowl mix the yolks and cream with the juice of a lemon. Pour a few spoonfuls of the thickened stock into the mixture. Off the heat, mix this sauce with the fish soup. Serve with fried croûtons. This is a very simple fish soup, perfectly satisfactory on its own. To make it more substantial add two more whiting fillets. Sprinkle with parsley or chervil.

SOUPE AU PISTOU
Bean Soup with Basil

Spanish Gazpacho and Pistou soup are to me ideal summer soups, redolent of Mediterranean flavours and aromas. Pistou soup has nothing of the smooth sophistication of a Vichyssoise, but it is full of sunshine and tells of easy, relaxed days. Each would suit a different atmosphere. Pistou soup, originally from Nice, once attached to the Italian peninsula, is very popular in the whole of Provence and the Mediterranée. It requires summer vegetables, but it would not exist without the Pistou sauce. Originally it was a mixture of fresh basil, garlic and olive oil. In Marseilles I saw it being made with bush basil. This type

of basil, with broad leaves, is used uncooked with salads and
sauces. *Pistou* comes from the Provençal word *Pesto*, meaning
pestle, and it is often used nowadays as meaning *basil*. Needless
to say, when I make the Pistou sauce I use a mixer! Basil can
be grown in pots, even in a northern climate, so the recipe is
suitable for all types.

For 5 to 6 people
2 litres/3½ pints water
Bouquet garni
3 small courgettes, diced
350 g/¾ lb French beans or tender runner beans, sliced
2—3 medium-sized, tender carrots, sliced
200 g/7 oz flageolet beans (soaked overnight)
2 small potatoes, cut into cubes
125 g/4½ oz short cut macaroni.
2 ripe tomatoes

PISTOU SAUCE
1 good size bunch of basil
4 good sized cloves of garlic
Olive oil to bind (3—4 spoonfuls)
80 g/3 oz freshly grated Parmesan, Gruyère or Pecorina

Drain and rinse the flageolet (soaked beforehand). Bring to the
boil in plenty of water. When the beans have cooked for 45 to
50 minutes, add the other vegetables (courgettes and potatoes
last), and season. Add the macaroni and cook for about 10
minutes or until just soft.

For the Pistou sauce, combine in the mixer the basil, chopped
garlic cloves, the cheese, and bind with olive oil. Add to the
soup. Check the seasoning (a good sprinkling of freshly ground
pepper). Serve and enjoy this hearty and tasty soup.

SOUPE DE POTIRON
Pumpkin Soup

In the autumn, a big colourful pumpkin cooked in the oven
is an instant success with a large family or guests, for an informal
evening. It is almost a meal in itself   19

For 8 to 10 people
300—500 g/10—16 oz Gruyère cheese (or Gouda, Cheddar or
  Parmesan)
Pumpkin 6—8lb
1—1½ pints single cream
4—6 slices toasted bread (crust removed), cut into cubes
3 leeks—white only, finely sliced and softened in a little oil and
  butter
Salt and freshly ground pepper

Cut the top off the pumpkin (the lid), remove the seeds and
fill the inside with the leeks, toasted bread, grated cheese, cream
and seasoning. With the lid on, cook in a hot oven (220C/425F/
mark 7) for just over two hours (depending on its size)—the
flesh should be soft but the outside must remain firm. The larger
pumpkins should be wrapped with protective foil, to prevent
possible sagging—it makes for easier handling too. When ready,
with a large spoon, scoop slices gently and evenly from the inside
walls of the pumpkin (make sure the walls do not become too
thin). Mix all the ingredients thoroughly and add some warm
light cream if it appears too thick; rectify the seasoning, and
Bon appétit! Next day more soup could be made with what is
left inside, adding creamy milk, seasoning and a sprinkling of
cheese.

CRÈME DE PETITS POIS À LA MENTHE
Cream of Garden Pea Soup

Here is rather a sophisticated soup made with *petits pois*. Sadly
nowadays fresh garden peas are rarely sold in the shops. Maybe
for the better since they do not keep well and too often I have
seen 'fresh' peas in a shop that looked yellow and past their
prime. In late spring, at school, after the evening meal, occasionally a few girls had to stay behind to shell the peas for the next
day—a boring but necessary job, and anyway they could always
eat a pod or two unnoticed.

The most usual recipe for this vegetable is *petits pois à la
française*. Without the stock it can be used as a vegetable. Add
enough liquid to the dish and it becomes a delicately flavoured
soup.

For 4 to 5 people
500 g/1 lb shelled peas (keep a few aside)
30 g/1 oz butter (or butter and oil)
1 small lettuce (shredded)
Thyme, mint
1 tbsp cream
1 tsp sugar
1 litre/1¾ pints chicken stock or water
150 g/5 oz spring onions
Salt and pepper

Fry the onions. Keep some of the green shoots to chop up and scatter on the soup before serving. Add the shredded lettuce, the peas, a pinch of thyme and cook slowly until tender. Season (add sugar if necessary). To make a soup, dilute with hot water or chicken stock. Cook for another 10 to 15 minutes and purée to make a nicely flavoured and coloured soup. Before serving, add a spoonful of cream to the soup. On each bowl sprinkle some finely chopped mint and add a spoonful of whole peas. It can be served hot or cold.

When peas get a little larger and more floury, add to each plate some puréed red pepper (grilled or fried) with or without cream. It is colourful and the flavours blend well.

Hors d'oeuvres

HORS D'OEUVRES

A good healthy *hors d'oeuvre* is often a prerequisite at the family table and in restaurants. The combinations and the seasonings are infinite and varied but simple.

Celeriac is easy to find in Britain. It is an excellent vegetable which can be served raw or cooked. Grated (not too finely) it is traditionally served at the beginning of a meal, mixed with mayonnaise, well flavoured with mustard, and called *céleri* CÉLERI *rémoulade*. The mixture is rather rich and can be thinned with REMOULADE yoghurt. A little horseradish instead of mustard, mixed with cream, is an alternative.

Cucumber sliced and sprinkled with salt beforehand has a CUCUMBER pleasant crunchiness and makes a good salad. Drain the cucum- SALAD ber before making the salad and use a light vinaigrette or a mix- ture of yoghurt, cream and dill. It is worth knowing that cucumber salted beforehand is easier to digest and does not repeat. Yoghurt added to cucumber has the same effect.

As a child, I liked to make a summer starter simple and colourful. Cut a good tomato, ripe and firm, into slices without cutting right through. It turns into a tomato accordion. Slice TOMATO a boiled egg and place between each tomato slice. Season before ACCORDION serving with a well-flavoured herb vinaigrette.

Grated vegetables are easy, healthy, colourful, and econo- CARROT mical. Carrots, beetroot (if uncooked slice particularly finely) BEETROOT and raw apples make a wonderfully colourful salad, mixed AND APPLE together or in 3 separate triangles. SALAD

Another imaginative *hors d'oeuvre*, using firm tomatoes to TOMATO make little baskets, is decorative enough to be served on special BASKETS occasions. Cut a handle in the round end of a tomato with a sharp knife. Scoop out carefully the inside of the tomato with a coffee spoon and a grapefruit knife, taking care not to pierce the skin. Sprinkle with a little salt and lay sideways to let the water run out. The choice of filling is yours, it can be simple or sophisticated. As a very young teenager, my recipe was basic: tinned tuna, drained and mixed with a lemony mayonnaise. Fill up each little basket, decorate with a touch of parsley, a caper or mayonnaise.

For stuffed eggs, an elderly friend of mine used finely chopped ham and chopped green olives bound with hard-boiled yolk of egg and mayonnaise. She was proud of this culinary prowess and said, her eyes sparkling with pride, 'This is my recipe!'. Replace the tuna with shrimps or salmon and vary the flavouring: prawn, crab or smoked salmon butter (bought in jars).

STUFFED
EGGS

Grilled and puréed red peppers with mayonnaise make a useful and versatile sauce for *hors d'oeuvre*. Cold salmon and red pepper mayonnaise bring a tasty change. Once visiting a French friend for lunch, I had *hors d'oeuvre* prepared with children in mind—pretend mushrooms that everybody wanted to eat; the basic ingredients are boiled eggs and tomatoes. Cook the eggs for at least 8 minutes in boiling water. They will be easier to fill as the yolks remain well-centred and the white uniformly set. Cut in two (the rounder end being the basis for the mushroom). Fill with your choice of mixture and top with a white cap (the cut-off top) coloured with specks of tomato purée. To look more real, colour this stem brown by dipping in chicory coffee. For a red cap, use a tomato top decorated with specks of white of egg stuck with a little mayonnaise. Nicely arranged on a bed of lettuce, saffron rice, or grated carrots, they look most appetising.

PRETEND
MUSHROOMS

SALADE DE LAITUE
Lettuce Salad

A lettuce freshly picked from the garden, together with a bunch of tarragon and a boiled egg, are the basis for a perfect salad. For seasoning make a well-balanced vinaigrette. Add a colourful sprinkling of boiled egg (using a small mouli grater) before serving. It is sheer perfection in its simplicity. In a *salad mimosa* only the yolk is used to sprinkle over the salad before it is brought to the table. I use both the white and the yolk, but separately, sprinkling the white outside and the yellow in the centre.

SALAD
MIMOSA

COCKTAIL DE PAMPLEMOUSSE
Grapefruit and Palm Hearts

When I left France for Britain a friend gave me this recipe; it is an easy, refreshing starter and I used it often.

For 6 people
3 large pink, juicy grapefruit cut in two
100 g/4 oz walnuts
200 g/7 oz prawns
1 large tbsp mayonnaise
1 tbsp lemon juice
1 tbsp cream or Greek yoghurt
500 g/1 lb tin of palm hearts (or 2 avocados)
Plenty of freshly ground pepper

Remove the flesh from the grapefruit in the usual way; do so over a bowl so as not to lose the juice. In a bowl, mix the grapefruit pieces, the prawns, the walnut pieces (if they do not taste fresh enough soak for 2 to 3 hours in salted water), the palm hearts cut into 2 or 3 pieces, or the avocado. The salad is better if it is served very cool. Just before serving, stir in the mayonnaise (with the cream or Greek yoghurt), the lemon juice and plenty of pepper and a little salt. Decorate with walnuts and prawns.

CAROTTES RAPÉES
Carrot Salad

For 3 to 4 people
½ kg/1 lb carrots
10 black olives
Garlic—to taste
Lemon juice

Chop the olives and marinate overnight with a little olive oil, crushed garlic and coriander—they will be more tasty. Grate the carrots quite coarsely and mix with all the ingredients. Alternatively just mix them with the oil and lemon juice and a small handful of sultanas.

TAPENADE
Savoury Caper Sauce

This is an old recipe from Provence, although originally it came from ancient Greece. It is a thick savoury paste and highly versatile.

For 6 to 8 people
200 g/7 oz black olives, stoned
100 g/4 oz well-drained capers
½ small tin of anchovies in oil
Garlic (optional)
Olive oil

Use a mixer for ease and rapidity and blend all the ingredients together using enough oil to make it into a thickish spread. Serve on small bits of toasted bread. It stimulates the appetite (and thirst). The tapenade I tried in Provence was thick, not especially smooth. The flavour was good and well balanced—very tasty but not pungent. It was no doubt made with excellent olives, the traditional way, pounded rather than quickly mixed. I find this Mediterranean recipe very useful. It keeps well in a cool place. (Add a little layer of oil if it has to keep for long).

One tablespoon of tapenade boosts a vinaigrette for a summer salad, tomatoes especially, or a mixed salad with tomatoes, cucumbers and egg quarters, for example. A spoonful of tapenade mixed with a small tin of tuna makes a good filling for eggs.

LAMB CHOPS   The paste can be spread thinly on lamb chops before grilling and served with grilled peppers, seasoned with vinaigrette. (Peppers grilled beforehand or parboiled are easier to digest). Giving a lift to everyday cooking is so important.

FONDUES DE PARMESAN

A tasty fritter to start the meal, or a main dish for a light dinner.

For 6 people
300 ml/½ pint milk
60 g/2 oz butter
120 g/4½ oz flour
2 eggs
120 g/4½ oz grated parmesan
Salt and pepper
Oil or vegetable fat
Home-made bread crumbs

Melt the butter, mix in the flour and stir. While it is cooking,
28 add the cold milk slowly and keep stirring. When the sauce has

thickened add the grated cheese. Stir until the mixture is cooked and leaves the sides of the pan, then take off the heat. Separate the yolks and mix into the cooling sauce. Spread this cream evenly on a well-oiled rectangular dish and let it cool completely. The mixture should be about half an inch thick. Divide into small squares or rectangles, roll in a little flour, then dip them in the whisked whites and roll well in the breadcrumbs. Fry in hot fat until golden and crunchy. Drain on kitchen paper. Serve immediately, perhaps with a well-seasoned Provençale tomato sauce or fried parsley, and a salad.

TERRINE DE LAPIN
Rabbit Terrine

Wild rabbit is plentiful and cheap. It gives a delicious flavour to pâtés and terrines, but it must be gutted as soon as it is caught unless you want a 'gamey' flavour. It is more popular in France than in Britain.

For 6 people
1 medium sized rabbit ($1\frac{1}{2}$ kg/2-3 lb)
500 g/1 lb coarsely minced pork shoulder
225 g/$\frac{1}{2}$ lb streaky bacon, as fat as possible
1 egg
1 large glass dry white wine
1 small glass brandy
Plenty of thyme, pepper and salt

Cut the meat off the legs and mince finely. Remove the meat from the saddle and slice finely. Let the slices marinate with the wine and thyme for a full hour. Mix the leg meat, pork shoulder and streaky bacon, all previously minced. (An obliging butcher will do it, which cuts down preparation time.) In a bowl mix the minced meats, the marinade, the brandy, seasonings; plenty of freshly-ground pepper is required to enhance the flavour and sharpen the appetite. The bacon is already salty but more salt may be required. It is worth checking the flavour before filling the terrine (fry a spoonful of the mixture). Fill the terrine in layers, (mincemeat then sliced saddle) finishing with a layer of minced meats and add a small bunch of thyme on top. If caul fat is available, cover the terrine with it for protec- 29

tion and appearance. At this point let it rest for an hour for
the flavour to develop. Cook in a warm oven in a *bain-marie*
for 90 minutes or so. Make sure, by using a fork, that the juices
from the terrine run clear, not pink. Cool the terrine for 24 hours
with a weight on top. With the bones, sliced onions, peppercorns and stock (or wine and water) make a tasty reduced
stock to add to the terrine while it is still warm. Serve with pickled chanterelles or home-made Cumberland sauce.

For a game terrine I sometimes make a Cumberland sauce
with red-currant berries rather than jelly. It gives a good texture. Jam made with red-currant berries is a change from jelly.
In the north of France, in Bar le Duc, there is a speciality: red-
currant jam with a difference and an incredible price tag. All
the pips have been carefully removed from each berry with a
toothpick, a fine knitting needle or a goose feather. Nuns did
this unrewarding task in the past. Two years ago this jam was
still prepared, as I saw in one or two specialist shops. This little
sophistication did not even stir my curiosity!

TERRINE DE PORC AU GENIÈVRE
Pork Terrine with Juniper

Until recently one could buy in France thrush pâté flavoured
with juniper, for these little birds like to feed on the aromatic
berries and their flesh acquires some of the flavour. Thrushes
are now protected and these pâtés have at last disappeared. In
the south I bought pork pâté with juniper; to replace the thrush
pâté, said the charcutier. It was quite excellent. Quite often I
have been reproached for the Europeans' habit of eating birds,
even sparrows. Once, in fact not so long ago, the scarcity and
the high price of meat made it out of reach of the rural popu-
lation. It then became a tradition to eat song birds but now it
is quite unnecessary, especially when birds are threatened by
man and the environment.

I like to gather juniper berries early in the autumn, on the
hills, be it Scotland or France. The easiest way to get them,
without too much scratching and high temper, is to shake the
branch into a plastic bag. Back home, empty the contents into
a large sieve. The prickly needles fall off and the dark blue berries remain. Kept in an air-tight jar, the aroma lingers beauti-

fully for a whole year. I find it wonderful with game.

For 6 to 8 people
500 g/1 lb pork belly
500 g/1 lb lean pork
1 slice ham
10—15 juniper berries, crushed beforehand
1 small glass of gin
1 large egg
1 tsp salt
Pepper

The terrine needs good seasoning, complementing without drowning the juniper flavour. Mix the meats, egg, gin, berries and seasoning. Fill the terrine, cover with a lid or foil, having added a few juniper berries on the top. Cook in a medium oven for at least an hour in a *bain-marie*. Cool until the next day, with something heavy on top.

Juniper often flavours sauerkraut. In the country, bakers burnt juniper in their ovens, it gave flavour and character to the bread. Why not try it for a barbecue?

PISSALADIÈRE
Onion and Anchovy Pie

The city of Nice finally cut its links with Italy in the middle of the last century. But the Italian flavours, like Pistou soup, lingered on and were soon enjoyed all over Provence. The Mediterranean is the common factor in those parts and influences everybody and everything. Pissaladière from the word *Pissalat* is a well-seasoned fish paste, essentially made with anchovies. This paste was brushed all over the tasty onion dish. Traditionally, like *pizzas* in Italy, *empanadas* in Spain or *quiches* in Lorraine, it was made with thin bread dough. Your local baker could provide it (as they do in France), though nowadays it is often made successfully with shortcrust pastry. Personally, I like the oil pastry mentioned at the beginning of the book as it is easy and good.

For 6 people
250 g/9 oz flour

31

1 glass (250 ml) equal mix of tepid water and olive oil. Whisk
 before adding to the flour for better blending.
Pinch of salt
750 g/1 ½ lb onions finely sliced
2 tbsp oil
Thyme and bay leaf
1 tin anchovies
100 g/4 oz good quality black olives

Mix the flour, water and oil, and salt to make a pastry. Roll
finely, line an oven dish (the quiche type, the sides need not
be fluted). Fry the onions gently until soft. Mix with half the
anchovies, finely chopped. Add half the stoned olives, also chopped. Cover the pastry with this highly flavoured onion mixture.
Do not add any salt. Decorate with the rest of the anchovy fillets
cut lengthwise and make a lattice effect with half olives arranged
in between. Sprinkle with a little oil and bake in a brisk heat
for 25 to 30 minutes. After 15 minutes reduce the heat if necessary. Serve warm as a starter or a main dish with a salad (good
tomatoes flavoured with basil or parsley), or cut into squares
and serve with a drink.

CHICKEN LIVERS

The best ones come from good free-range birds fed on grain.
Otherwise try to get those sold by a supplier who deals with
fresh birds.

FOIES DE POULET AUX ÉPINARDS
Chicken Livers with Raw Spinach

Marinate the livers in milk for at least one night. It does mellow
the flavour. Quite often, for good measure, I add a little Muscat
wine. Medium sherry would be equally good. Cut the livers
into two, roll in flour and fry in hot butter on all sides (if the
heat is too fierce there is a lot of dangerous spitting). Reduce
the heat and cover with a lid. Do not overcook; the insides must
be still pink. It is a good way of testing. Season with salt and
pepper and a little nutmeg. Mix with the tender leaves of some
raw spinach. Add garlicky croutons and walnuts. This salad is
32 not only tasty, but colourful and very healthy. Instead of using

ordinary vinaigrette, be more adventurous: deglaze the frying pan with cider vinegar (2 tbsp). Off the heat add some pouring cream, season, and pour over the salad.

DES OEUFS POUR TOUS LES GOÛTS
Eggs for any taste

In late spring, at sunset, when the country lanes were filled with the scent of wild honeysuckle, fetching the milk from the farm was a popular errand.

One Sunday evening I was later than usual and the farmer's wife had gone to her kitchen. There the family was sitting round the table for the evening meal. They were eating eggs which were piled in a basket, and, like our early ancestors probably did in their caves, sucking them raw. The custom must have been widespread in the past if one believes the old saying, *You cannot teach your granny to suck eggs!* The farmer in particular attracted my attention—he sucked his eggs noisily, efficiently and with obvious relish. *À chacun son goût*; tolerance in all things, I say, forty years later. At seven or eight years old I probably thought otherwise.

These people have left the area, the farm buidings have gone and by now the memory is getting blurred. But the incident singled out the man for ever. To this day, I remember his nickname, his ungainly gait, plain round face, and baggy trousers gathered at the waist held by a brown belt.

This scene did not improve my opinion of eggs. To make up for my lack of appetite at breakfast time, my anxious mother devised a *menu énergie* that should keep me going and give her peace of mind on a cold and frosty morning. The recipe is simple; take an egg, very fresh of course, break it and separate with great care the yolk from the white. Whisk the yolk with a cup of hot milk sweetened to taste. It is most nourishing, ideal for convalescents, children and elderly people. But the combination of strong-tasting eggs and good creamy milk soon became too much for my tender taste buds. Mother changed the recipe to coffee and egg, but it was not a treat since I was not allowed strong coffee, and it was never very hot anyway. Daily I swallowed the mixture with clenched teeth watched by an anxious but inflexible mother. Occasionally, a jeering older brother, annoyed by my protests and grimaces, threatened to hold my nose and pour the coffee down my throat!

Eggs became acceptable only when I acquired a craving for large sun-ripe tomatoes, sliced and fried with garlic and parsley. Eggs smothered in this tasty colourful sauce soon became a favourite summer dish. This did not surprise a Portuguese friend, who quoted a saying from his country, *There are no bad cooks with tomatoes.* How much poorer European cooking must have been before Cristobel Colon and his discovery of the Americas! While agreeing with the saying, I must add that tomatoes with everything is wrong as well, especially when tomatoes mean tomato purée.

OMELETTE PAYSANNE
Rustic Omelette

This makes a good supper dish served simply with a green salad. It is ideal for picnics since it is just as good cold. Cut into mouth-sized bites, it is a tasty and easily made appetizer to serve with drinks. Several types of appetizers served with a drink before the meal can replace the first course and let the cook/hostess give all her attention to the main course. I believe such titbits, *amuse-gueule* or *amuse-bouche*, are imperative with drinks before a meal.

For 4 to 5 people
6—8 eggs
Oil
Salt and pepper
1 medium sized onion (sliced or chopped finely)
1 mild pepper (grilled or fried)
225 g/8 oz potatoes (chopped into small cubes)

Fry the onions until coloured, add the chopped pepper. If the pepper is grilled, simply add at the last minute. Put aside and keep warm. Fry the potatoes very slowly in the same pan, this is the secret of potato omelette. Add extra oil if necessary. When they are soft and nicely coloured, cook more gently with a lid on and season. Whisk the eggs briskly, but not too long. Cook

34

the omelette in a clean pan (non-stick preferably). When the eggs are just beginning to set, spread all the vegetables over them. Reduce the heat and cook on both sides until nicely coloured. Use a large dish (the size of the pan) to turn over the omelette. A little butter rubbed over the omelette gives a shiny finish.

This omelette is good made with lean smoked bacon, de- rinded and cut into small cubes. Best bacon as it is understood in Britain uses the loins and that is why it is so good and why the French love bacon and eggs when they come to Britain.

'Le bacon' is a French word from the medieval days. As we distinguish between pig and pork, the French distinguish between *le cochon* and *le porc salé* or *le bacon*. To make sure the bacon is not too salty, blanch for a minute or two and then fry. For an omelette the bacon must be sliced more thickly than for bacon and eggs.

For 4 people
6—8 eggs
Pepper
Lean bacon, thickly sliced and cut into cubes
1—2 tbsp of lard (or oil and lard—use the fat rendered by the
  bacon)

Grill or fry the bacon. Cook the omelette, adding the bacon. Fold and serve. To make this omelette more substantial a cooked potato chopped and fried with the bacon can be added.

OEUFS BOURGUIGNONNE
Eggs in a Red Wine Sauce

Oeufs Bourguignonne, vigneronne, or *en meurette* are poached eggs in a red wine sauce. They are served on fried bread, garlicky preferably. It is the best way to turn anybody into an egg lover. I have been a witness to several conversions. The recipe originated in a vine growing area, probably Burgundy, with plenty of red wine, eggs, imagination, a love of cooking and a spirit of economy. A similar red wine sauce is used with freshwater fish and the flavour is splendid. Personally, though, the thought of tiny fish bones makes me feel uneasy. (In a French restaurant *Moules Bourguignonne* in red wine, a change from *Moules* 35

Marinière, were unexpected but surprisingly good.)

No need for a vintage wine for this recipe; use a good red wine with body. In vine growing areas they even use the *lees* of the wine (the deposit at the bottom of the barrel); for me, it is rather rich.

The sauce can be cooked beforehand; it is even better reheated. Any surplus kept in the deep-freeze is welcome when the larder is low and plainly poached eggs have no appeal.

For 4 people
4 very fresh eggs
½ litre/1 pint red wine
3 cloves garlic
Pinch of thyme
1 bay leaf
4 or 5 parsley stems
1 lump of sugar (1 level tsp)
4 slices bread
Salt and pepper
1/4 lb streaky bacon, chopped, added early on to the wine mixture (optional)
1/4 lb sliced mushrooms, fried and added before serving (optional)

As is the case with lots of traditional recipes, there are variations. This is possibly the easiest. Boil the wine with the herbs, the shallots, garlic and sugar on a gentle heat for 20 minutes or so. The lengthy cooking and the touch of sugar removes any possible acidity. By then the sauce should have reduced by almost half. Sieve, and push through the solids with a wooden spoon. Keep the sauce warm and add *beurre manié* just before serving.

BEURRE MANIÉ

30 g flour
30 g butter

Beurre manié is always used for thickening a sauce. Mix thoroughly the flour and the creamy butter. It should not become too solid. Add more butter if necessary. Add to the hot sauce, stirring on a very low heat. Remove from the heat (do not cook anymore after that point), rectify the seasonings and keep warm. The butter makes the sauce smooth and mellow.

FRIED BREAD, TWO METHODS
One slice per person without the crust.

1. To get a rather potent garlic flavour, toast the bread and rub the garlic clove on one side (the rough surface acts as a grater).
2. In a frying pan with oil or oil and butter add 2 to 3 cloves of garlic, fry gently. When the garlic is soft remove from the pan and fry the bread in the flavoured oil.

POACHING THE EGGS

Use very fresh eggs—they taste better and poach more easily. Bring to the boil a pan of water with 1 or 2 dessertspoons of wine added. The water must be shivering, *frémissante*. Poach one egg at a time and, when cooked—2 to 4 minutes according to taste, remove with a slotted spoon onto absorbent paper.

In a large shallow dish arrange the bread with one (or two) poached eggs on top, cover with the sauce and serve straightaway, while hot. It is an ideal recipe at any time of the year as a starter or a light meal. The wine sauce is full of flavour, but without alcohol; it all went in fumes in the early stages of the cooking; it would be an ideal dish for vegetarians.

Oeufs en meurette is similar but more elaborate. The sliced onions are fried in a little oil and butter, the spoonful of flour is stirred in and cooked briefly, then add the wine, sugar, herbs, chopped bacon and cook as before. Before serving whisk in a little butter. OEUFS EN MEURETTE

QUICHE

When the quiche explosion was in full swing in Britain there were quiches everywhere, and of every kind. As far as I was concerned, there were two varieties: the good ones and the others, and a world of difference between them. A good quiche has a perfectly cooked pastry base and a tasty, creamy filling.

It is believed that quiches originated in Lorraine in the north of France a long time ago. On bread making days any left-over dough was rolled thinly and cooked with a filling of cream, yolks 37 and bacon—all things found easily in a northern country kitchen. Nowadays there are quiches, or rather savoury flans, everywhere and with a variety of fillings. Bread dough has been replaced by shortcrust pastry, or even puff pastry for the most delicate ones. The mixture of cream and yolks is rather rich for our diets; creamy milk, strained yoghurt or quark with eggs and bacon makes a pleasant, lighter combination. For delicate preparations, instead of using three eggs I use two yolks and two whole eggs. It all looks very simple, but there are many trials and errors in producing a good quiche.

A good oven of even temperature and good baking ware are the starting points. The traditional quiche dish is supposed to have fluted sides. It is pretty but not essential. When I have time in hand I prefer to bake the pastry first for 15 minutes at 190C/375F/mark 5 for shortcrust pastry and 200C/420F/mark 6 for puff pastry, using cold pastry. (Put shortcrust in the fridge and the puff pastry into the freezing compartment, for 30 minutes or so). Cook the pastry blind. When this is done, add the filling and bake for a further 25 minutes also, bringing the temperature down to 155C/325F which is ideal for the egg mixture. If by this time the filling is not quite set, switch off the oven and leave the quiche inside.

SHORTCRUST PASTRY

260 g/9 oz flour
125 g/4½ oz butter (or mixed with vegetable oil)
Pinch of salt
A little water to bind

TRADITIONAL QUICHE FILLING

150 g/5 oz lean bacon, cut into cubes and blanched
3 eggs and 1 yolk
350 ml/12 fl. oz creamy milk (or 2/3 milk with 1/3 cream)

QUICHE AU SAUMON FUMÉ
Smoked Salmon Quiche

This is an easy dish and looks rather good and sophisticated, using cheaper cuts of smoked salmon.

For 6 people
250 g/½ lb puff pastry
250 g/½ lb broccoli
150 g/5 oz smoked salmon, chopped
3 eggs and 1 yolk
400 ml/14 fl.oz creamy milk
Salt and pepper to taste

Line a quiche dish (20–22 cm/9–10 inches) with the pastry, rolled thinly. Prick with a fork and bake blind. Meanwhile blanch the broccoli, using only tender florets. Drain. Spread the broccoli (just tender) and the cheaper cuts of smoked salmon onto the pastry base. Prepare the creamy egg mixture, season if necessary, pour over the salmon and broccoli and bake in the oven for a good 25 minutes

This same recipe can be used for many varieties of quiche: spinach, leeks, prawns, tomatoes with bacon and cheese, onion and pepper. Cheese, herbs and onions can be added to some of them or simply cheese on its own. The varieties are endless. Over to you!

Saucisse
de Toulouse

SAUCISSE DE TOULOUSE

Charcuterie is an old and well established tradition in France,
It started with the Gauls, wild pigs, an abundance of acorns
in the forest, and the Romans turned gastronomic instructors.
If not a fashionable sight, pigs roaming the streets of Paris were
a normal one up to the fifteenth century. They became such
a nuisance that the king had to ban them from his capital, no
doubt disappointing many enterprising gourmets. His son and
heir, the Dauphin, died in an accident when his chariot met
with some of these wanderers. Times have changed and so has
the way of life, the diet, the economy. A few farmers still take
the trouble of rearing a pig for the family. When they do, they
attach great importance to quality and tradition. During my
autumn pilgrimage to the south I had a conducted tour of a
friend's farm, a prosperous blend of modern and traditional.
We came to a pen with two lively pigs: one for the household,
the other for the son who lived and worked in the town. I very
much approved of that town and country association.

I have watched the making of these sausages in an old-
fashioned *charcuterie* run by a tiny but formidable widow,
always impeccably dressed in black clothes, her hair neatly
gathered in a chignon. Cleanliness went hand in hand with
godliness, the latter emanating from the proprietor's spinster
sister, quiet and subdued like a Carmelite nun. (Her fiancé, I
heard it said, never returned from *La Grande Guerre*.) The
owner retired at eighty two, reluctant to let down her customers.
The flow of tempting and tasty charcuteries came to an end
but not without a grand finale, *tradition oblige*. All the treasures
of a *charcuterie de campagne* were there. Over the years I had
sampled them all—*saucisse* of all kinds, even saucisse with truf-
fles at Christmas; *saucissons* (salamis); pâtés cut in wedges that
looked and smelt irresistible; black pudding for its enthusiasts;
cooked hams and raw hams, *jambon de campagne*, the *jambons*
requiring lengthy and careful supervision. When ready to eat,
they were cut in thickish slices that give all the flavour in a
mouthful. Parma hams made the more dainty and sophisticated
morsels.

The older generation used to say that every part of the pig could be eaten, hooves and bristle excepted. A non-throwaway mentality, out of necessity and out of care too. They made *fritons* or *grattons*, little known nowadays outside the more traditional rural areas. Once the fat is chopped, with bits of meat left in it, it is melted slowly and sieved; the residue, while hot, is sprinkled liberally with salt and pepper, and eaten cold like *rillettes*. Goose or duck *fritons* are much more tasty but more expensive, obviously. In the farms of the past when the family pig was turned into winter reserves, the melting of the lard was the grandmother's task. The quality and whiteness depended on the gentle cooking. Vivid in my memory is the figure of an old woman sitting by the fire and keeping an eye on the copper pot and the melting fat. Where it was, or who she was, I have long forgotten. I fear modern dieticians would not approve of *fritons*, or most *charcuterie* for that matter. One should simply avoid what a 17th century book from our home library, *The Family Physician*, keeps mentioning over and over again, namely: 'exce*ff*'. Nowadays we talk about moderation, but common sense is of all ages.

Getting a kitchen of my own was a big step in my married life. There I was free and could cook what I wanted, and forget about mince cooked in water, instant sauces, trifles with solid custard, jelly and so on. The honeymoon period at the table had been brief, except for those lovely afternoon teas and puddings enriched with the best cream—*crème fleurette* as it is known in France. It was skimmed from the large milk pans kept in the dairy. The resident cow was fed on good lush grass in the warm season; in winter, to boost her diet, she munched through cabbages from the vegetable garden.

But such luxuries did not make me forget about all those other flavours I was beginning to miss terribly—and among them, Saucisses de Toulouse, well-seasoned, chunky, full of flavour and so different from the ones found in Britain. One look around Europe, and it is obvious that Britain, Spain, Italy, Germany, Switzerland, Poland, in fact all of them have sausages of their own, some cooked, others smoked or dried, flavoured with garlic, paprika, hot pepper, cumin, fennel or sage. The idea is the same but the variations are infinite.

We had with us for a while a very nice and interesting English helper. She was just back from France, the Lyon area, after spending a couple of years working for a world health organisation. Naturally, in the kitchen and at the table we talked a lot about food and cooking, similarities and differences. Lyon is well known for its great choice of sausages and their excellence. 'Surely', I said rashly, 'with such a choice, nobody would have missed the British sausage'. 'Not so', she replied with a big grin, 'anyone going home for a holiday was begged to bring back English bangers!'

Do *sausages* encapsulate for each individual away from home the flavour of his country or province? After all, it is one of the first savoury flavours tried at a young age and that is important!

SAUCISSES DE TOULOUSE
Toulouse Sausages — as I make them in Scotland

These are easy and economical and should be highly seasoned. It is essential that pepper is used liberally. The pork I buy from the butcher is lean and young (quite different from fat bacon pigs). Half pork belly and half pork shoulder make the right mixture for very lean sausages. Two parts of fat pork to one of lean pork make fattier ones. The meat is minced with the large blade of the mincer. It looks and tastes better; originally the chopping was done by hand. The salt and pepper are an early way of preserving the meat, and they flavour pork admirably. An old coffee grinder kept for spices grinds the peppercorns quickly and not too finely.

500 g/1 lb pork belly
500 g/1 lb pork shoulder
1 dsp salt—slightly rounded and preferably sea-salt
1 level tsp freshly ground pepper, or more to taste
1 glass red or white wine

Mix the meat and seasoning thoroughly in a bowl, cover and let the flavours develop in a cool place for a couple of hours. The addition of a glass of wine, red or white, was usual in the country. Putting the meat into skins is always done by the 45 butcher; he has the experience, the equipment and my grateful thanks. Without his help the whole operation would be too lengthy and finicky. Plump or thin, these sausages are made into one long coil like the Cumberland type. A string of sausages is known as *un chapelet de saucisses*—a rosary!

COOKING THE SAUSAGES.

A barbecue brings out the best, sending out tempting messages all around. It is going back to roots, country cooking, simple and tasty. Served with a green salad and baked potatoes, it makes an easy and pleasant meal. The sausages need 8 to 10 minutes cooking. If they are tightly filled, pricking all over with a fine needle avoids bursting.

CARGOLADE A Catalan friend of mine used to talk about Easter picnics near Perpignan. Family and friends went for the *cargolade*, i.e. grilling sausages and snails, boosted with a spicy mayonnaise, and no doubt plenty of local wine. That custom would not, or could not, easily catch on in Scotland! Traditionally these spicy, chunky sausages are eaten with a potato puree—bangers and mash with a difference. It is simple cuisine without frills but with plenty of followers.

PURÉE DE POMME DE TERRE
Potato Purée

Potatoes
Milk
Butter
Salt and pepper
2 or 3 tbsp Gruyère or Emmenthal cheese, grated

When I want a light and fluffy purée I use an old-fashioned mouli-légume, the medium blade. Very hot potatoes and hot milk are essential for best results. Add the milk a little at a time, to reach the desired consistency, which should never be too dry or too sticky. A firm and steady wrist handling a potato masher is a good alternative. Seasoning and butter are added to taste. A sprinkling of Gruyère cheese or Emmenthal, coloured under the grill or in a hot oven for a minute or so, make it even more special, and a favourite with children, with its golden gratinée crust.

PURÉE DE CHOU ET POMMES DE TERRE
Cabbage and Potato Purée

SAUCISSE
DE TOULOUSE

Served with sausages this makes a light and interesting alternative.

1 medium-sized cabbage
500 g/1 lb potatoes
Salt and pepper
Cream—2 or 3 spoonfuls

Chop the cabbage coarsely, removing core and hard stalks, cook for up to fifteen minutes in boiling salted water until soft. Purée the cabbage. Cook the potatoes separately, mash and mix with the cabbage. Add pepper and more salt if necessary and some light cream to improve the flavour and smoothness.

Carrots, brussel sprouts and celeriac can be used in the same way (but with potatoes making only one third of the mixture). The vegetables must cook separately, the flavour is better.

At school, in winter time, we used to have sausages served with split pea purée. It makes a colourful, tasty, hearty dish; SPLIT PEA
PURÉE some croutons fried in butter (or butter and oil) add a crunchy touch. Soak the peas overnight in a cool place, start them in cold water, seasoned with salt, a bay leaf or two, two garlic cloves, one onion stuck with a clove. Bring to the boil then simmer for at least two hours until they become puréed.

CHOU BRAISÉ
Braised cabbage

1 medium-sized cabbage
1 onion
1 carrot
1 thick slice of streaky bacon, cut into cubes
3 tbsp oil

Slice the cabbage into strips (1 cm wide) removing tough leaves and thick stalks; cook in boiling water for 3 minutes, drain. Fry gently the chopped onion with the chopped carrot and the bacon. When the mixture begins to soften add the cabbage, season with a little salt and pepper, cook on a very low heat 47

until tender for 40 minutes with a lid on. When cooking cabbage
I tend to use freshly ground pepper quite lavishly, an addiction
I fear. This is the old-fashioned recipe with lengthy cooking.
The same recipe is good but different with shorter cooking: 15
minutes.

SAUCISSES AU VIN BLANC
Sausages in White Wine

500 g/1 lb sausages

1 chopped onion
2 tbsp oil
1 glass dry white wine
1 level tbsp flour

Fry the sausages with a little oil or lard, then keep aside in a
warm place. Add finely chopped onion to the pan (there should
be enough fat). Fry gently until soft, sprinkle with flour, cook
for a few seconds, stirring well and add the wine. The sauce
thickens quickly. Cook slowly for a few minutes, adding a little
water if necessary. For a really fast sauce you could alternatively
deglaze the frying pan with a glass of wine and a spoonful of
tomato purée which makes an instant and easy sauce. If it is
slightly acid add a pinch of sugar.

SAUCISSES À LA PROVENÇALE
Sausages Provencal Style

In summertime tomatoes give the sausages a new appeal. It is
a different approach—winter cooking turned into summer
cooking but always at the everyday level.

For 5 to 6 people
500 g/1 lb sausages
5—6 good sized tomatoes, the bigger the better
3—4 tbsp olive oil
1 tbsp chopped parsley
2 cloves garlic chopped very fine
1 tbsp homemade breadcrumbs
Salt and pepper

Fry the sausages all over in a little of the oil. Lard is more tradi- tional, olive oil is more digestible and gives more of a Provençal flavour. Arrange them in a shallow oven dish, a pottery dish looks in keeping with this type of cooking. Prepare the tomatoes: with a sharp knife cut off the top third of each tomato (use for soup later). The rest is fried for 2 or 3 minutes on each side, cut side down first. The heat should not be too brisk. Arrange the tomatoes around the sausages. Mix the garlic, some of the parsley and breadcrumbs and spread on the tomatoes, a good thickness. Dribble a little oil over each one. Let it cook and colour in a hot oven for a few minutes. Sprinkle with the rest of the parsley just before serving.

When tomatoes are too small, to avoid overcooking and disappointment, I fry the mixture separately and add to the cooked tomatoes before serving. Tantalising smells fill the kitchen instantly. In the frying pan pour 3 tablespoons oil; before the pan gets too hot add the chopped parsley then the garlic and last, the breadcrumbs; keep stirring until the mixture turns pale gold, which happens quickly. The garlic must not be allowed to brown, it becomes bitter. These garlicky tomatoes are also delicious served with a roast, chops etc.

In summer I like home-made *ratatouille* with the sausages. Before serving I add to the *ratatouille* a good spoonful of tomato purée for thickening and plenty of freshly-chopped basil.

COOKING WITH SAUSAGE MEAT

The butcher needs only to mince the meat, not stuff it. This home-made spicy sausage mixture can be adapted to hot or cold weather cooking. Use it for tasty stuffed cabbages or potatoes in January, and delicious stuffed tomatoes, courgettes, peppers or even squid in summer. Scottish style, it makes very good Scotch eggs or sausage rolls, known as *friands* in France. Served with a hot smooth sauce (tomato improved with wine or white wine, cream and onion, or mushroom) the *friands* take a different character with new possibilities.

CRÉPINETTES À L'ÉCOSSAISE

Accurately but unimaginatively, *crépinettes* could be called flat 49

sausages or sausages in an envelope. Since obtaining caul fat
or *crépine* proves almost impossible, I use streaky bacon instead,
To approach the lightness, the cobweb effect of caul fat, I flatten
each slice with a rolling pin in between two sheets of greaseproof
paper.

CRÉPINETTES, SIMPLE VERSION

Use at least 100 g/4 oz sausage mixture per person, give it the
shape of a plump beef burger, wrap in the thin bacon and cook
for 5 minutes on each side (grill, fry or barbecue).

For a more colourful version of *crépinettes* add to ½ kilo of
sausage meat one finely chopped medium-sized onion and one
tablespoon of finely chopped parsley. It is the version encoun-
tered in most French charcuteries. Imagination and preference
can vary the mixture almost *ad infinitum*, with chives, coriander,
crushed juniper, cumin, grilled pepper etc, adding, on creative
days, a sauce in keeping with the chosen flavour. These *crépinettes* can be grilled, fried, cooked with a wine or even a beer sauce.
Occasionally, for grilling, I use foil instead of bacon: they
become *saucisses en armure* (sausages in armour). Make each
parcel with 100 g or so of sausage meat, add one or two bay
leaves per parcel. Use plenty of foil to enclose the sausage meat.
It must be large enough and tight enough to hold in the *crépinettes*, the juices and the aroma. Cook under a hot grill, or barbecue
for about 10 to 12 minutes; over-cooking dries up the meat.
It is a simple recipe but very tasty, easy and aromatic.

Stuffed tomatoes evoke summer cooking *par excellence*, easy,
relaxed, full of flavour and sunshine. They are a must in the
south of France when tomatoes are at their best at the height
of the summer: big, firm, ripe, tasty, the same which make the
best tomato salads. A few years ago a young French friend spent
a few happy weeks with us. Chatting about this and that, I asked
her one day what she missed most in Britain, 'Tomatoes Farcies
and melons', she sighed. These tomatoes are eaten all over
France; the southern version is more special, more flavoured;
the best are home-grown. Twenty years ago Scottish tomatoes
produced in the greenhouse were too small to make *Tomates
Farcies*. Nowadays with a greater variety of imports, the size
is better. Beef tomatoes are in theory ideal, but they need a lot

of boosting to make up for their poor flavour and texture, the result of forcing in the greenhouses. With the traditional recipe I serve a well flavoured tomato sauce and it gives a good approximation of the southern stuffed tomatoes. Cold, they can be eaten on a picnic—and even grey skies do not matter so much, especially with a good Rosé de Provence, nicely cooled. Little streams make ideal wine coolers!

TOMATES FARCIES MÉRIDIONALES
Stuffed Tomatoes

For 6 people
1 large tomato per person
400 g sausage meat
2 slices stale bread, crumbled
1 large egg or two small ones
3 cloves garlic, finely chopped
1 small bunch chopped parsley
3—4 tbsp oil
Salt and pepper

Cut the top off the tomatoes (the stalk end) and keep aside. Scoop out the flesh with a spoon without piercing the skin, leaving a reasonable thickness all round. Sprinkle with salt and leave upside down for an hour. Mix all the ingredients together and fill each tomato generously with the sausage meat. Replace the 'caps', arrange in a large oven dish with the oil. Cook for 35 to 40 minutes in a moderately hot oven (204c/400F/mark 6). While the tomatoes are cooking, make the sauce.

SAUCE AUX TOMATES
Tomato sauce

2 tbsp tomato purée
1 small chopped onion
1 clove garlic
1 tbsp oil
Scooped out tomato flesh
$\frac{1}{2}$ glass wine

51

Chop the onion finely, fry and add the garlic and the chopped
tomato flesh; cook gently for 20 minutes, add the tomato purée
with the wine to thicken and flavour. Serve the tomatoes with
the sauce. For more sophistication, purée the sauce before
adding to the tomatoes. When there is plenty of parsley available
it can be deep fried in oil which is not too hot. It quickly turns
crisp and feathery. Dry on absorbent paper, sprinkle with salt
and arrange around the tomatoes. A dish high in colour and
flavour.

Cassoulet

CASSOULET

What is it all about? When I think of 'le Cassoulet', its glory
and its legend, I am not too nostalgic, and I should be. A
betrayal of my origins no doubt! Down south my friends would
say, with a shrug, that I had become *très Anglaise*. But my
enthusiasm is subdued. I cannot boast the robust and solid
appetite required to appreciate such a dish and do it justice.
My native area is a bastion of Gallic rugby: team spirit,
togetherness and enthusiasm are what is needed for a true
appreciation of le Cassoulet, with plenty of good local wine to
help it down, naturally.

Over the years, this hearty dish has become elaborate and
incredibly rich. It embodies the best of country traditions from
days gone by. Every region, even micro-region, in the Carcas-
sonne, Toulouse, Castelnaudary triangle owns 'the unique
recipe'. The Castelnaudary recipe may be more ancient, but
they are all worthy of praise. The *Larousse Gastronomique* refers
to it as 'the acknowledged trinity' of the Cassoulet—a very
French state of affairs, that gave rise to lively polemics in the
not so distant past. Wisdom has prevailed and a *modus vivendi*
has been reached.

White beans make its basis. *Charcuteries* and a variety of
meats make its excellence. The slow and lengthy cooking gives
the dish its smoothness and unctuosity.

My first attempt at Cassoulet in Britain was not a success.
It was years ago, when I was very green and very keen, unaware
that some dishes need their own special atmosphere to succeed.
A small, slightly formal, dinner party, with nearly new friends,
dainty appetites and a glint of silver was no setting for cassoulet.
My efforts at authenticity went unnoticed: imported goose fat,
coco beans and goose preserve were of no avail. Recently one
of my friends was extolling the virtues of a cassoulet 'made in
Britain' enjoyed by a group of congenial friends one winter
evening. My enthusiasm was revived, and I gave the Cassoulet
another try.

Making the dish as it should be made becomes, in this
country, a labour of love and a challenge, but it can be done 55

in instalments, without panic. On the day itself, the dish cooks gently and needs little supervision. Being such a rich combination, plenty of guests can be gathered for this 'one dish menu' — *un plat unique*. A couple of pineapples, ripe and fragrant, Kirsch optional, would be a perfect ending to the meal. Besides, their digestive virtues are a worthwhile consideration, French liver or not.

Some of the ingredients are easily found in this country but others may have to be specially made, such as the spicy pork rind rolls, the *confit* (pork preserve), the salt bacon and the pork sausages which should be chunky and spicy (like the Toulouse type)—they can be made ahead and kept in the freezer for a couple of weeks. Fresh Italian sausages, if available, are a good alternative.

SPICY PORK RIND ROLLS

Buy 225 g/½ lb pork rind. Be sure it is smooth; if not (as is often the case here) get rid of any unpleasant bristle with a flame or a camping gas or spirit lamp. Cut into strips, 5 to 6 cm wide (2 to 2½ inches) and twice the length. Season with salt, pepper, crushed garlic, and a little thyme. Roll and hold secure with kitchen string. These tasty, spicy bundles would add extra flavour and texture to many slow cooking casseroles at little expense. My mother used to buy from our charcuterie, a sausage made half and half with meat and chopped rind. It was full of flavour and bite and called *andouille*, nothing to do with the

ANDOUILLE *andouilles* of Vire.

CONFIT DE PORC
Pork preserve

A deep freeze cannot replace this ancient and tasty way of keeping pork. It keeps up to 6 months, at least, in a cool place and is ready to use within minutes for a variety of succulent dishes. The cooking is lengthy, but it is simple and satisfying to make; going back to the roots again, and with renewed pleasure.

Buy lean pork (loin is best though not essential). Bacon pigs, if available, are ideal as they mature and have more flavour than the ones sold usually at the butchers. Being a purist is not always possible unfortunately, but quality is still in the mind.

Prepare pieces of $\frac{1}{2}$ to 1 kilo/1 to 2 lbs meat. To be worth it, make plenty and keep for later use. Rub the meat all over with coarse sea salt. For extra flavour (optional) add thyme and a crushed bay leaf to the salt. Keep in a cool place. 24 hours later wipe the pieces carefully to remove all the salt and cook very slowly in good quality lard for 90 minutes or so. Do check with a long needle, the juices must run clean, but avoid over-cooking, the meat would become tough and dry. It is a slow form of deep frying, gentle and lengthy; a little bag with two or three cloves of garlic and peppercorns in the lard adds a southern touch, welcome in the case of young pork. For better, gentle and even cooking, use a deep pan, with a thick base. In the French farms of the past, brass cauldrons were used. They are similar to the brass jelly pans, but much bigger. *Brocanteurs* or bric-a-brac shops seem to have gathered many, for the benefit of the passing tourist with a secondary residence in the country.

The confit is kept in round-bellied earthenware jars, with a wide opening for easy access. In Britain, similar jars were used for preserving eggs—a less exciting content. My mother's generation was still very proud of the row of jars in the larder. It was a cheerful and reassuring gathering of treasures at the beginning of winter—as important as the huge pile of logs neatly stacked outside.

HOW TO KEEP THE PRESERVE:

When the cooking is over, pour some melted lard in the bottom of the jar and when it is set, add the meat and cover the lot with melted fat. There must be a good layer on the top (5 cm/2 inches or so). It is an insulation that guarantees the perfect keeping of the meat. Cover the pot with grease-proof paper—like a giant jam jar (plus lid if available).

PETIT SALÉ
Salt Pork

It is easy to find in Britain and very easy to make at home if you feel inclined; it is tasty and most useful in winter time. Use pork belly or other cheap cuts ($\frac{1}{2}$ to 1 kg/1 to 2 lbs), rub and cover with coarse sea salt for three days (in a pyrex dish of suitable size). Keep in a cool place . For such a relatively short spell I do not add saltpetre or sugar. When ready, wipe off all the salt and keep in the fridge wrapped in grease-proof paper (1 week to 10 days).

Before adding to the beans, soak the salt bacon in water for up to 2 hours. This *petit salé* is most useful in winter to add-flavour to quick dishes. Parboiled and cut into cubes it is delicious for quiches, saute potatoes, terrines, vegetables and salads.

To make a substantial green salad, grill or fry the parboiled *petit salé* under a good heat. Remove when it is well coloured, add the hot fat to the salad and deglaze the pan with 3 spoonfuls of vinegar (off the heat). It will add sharpness to the salad, whether it is potato, chicory, dandelion or raw spinach. One poached egg per person can be served with the salad and the crisp bacon; it is traditional, substantial and a very tasty and quick dish for winter or early spring. *Chapons* (cubes of dried bread rubbed with garlic) add more crunch and flavour—a good, well flavoured vinaigrette can replace hot fat, but it must be mixed in, half an hour before to soften the vegetables.

THE MAKING OF THE CASSOULET

There are variations, like any other well-tried and well-liked recipe. Mine is based partly on the *Larousse Gastronomique*, what I remember of early days, and more recent visits and chats with friends, and last but not least, the influence on me of my years in Britain. Beans are the basic ingredients. No beans, no Cassoulet. In the past small quantities were measured in volume. Pre-packing came with a more affluent society.

As a small child I used to go shopping with my mother and enjoyed the liveliness in the shops, and the light gossip. I remember the older generation buying sausage or black pudding by the length. A 'pan' was a good portion for one. It is the distance between the thumb and small finger when the hand is stretched. All the measures sounded very evocative and friendly.

For 10 to 12 people
700 g/1½ lbs white beans (or 1 litre)
700 g/1½ lbs sausages
225 g/½ lb pork rind
225 g/½ lb good garlic sausage

700 g/1½ lbs pork (or goose or duck) preserve
300 g/10 oz salt pork
700 g/1½ lbs fresh roast pork or lamb, if preferred. The lamb
   is improved with 3 extra cloves of garlic, sliced and spiked
   into the meat.
A bouquet garni (1 bay leaf, thyme, parsley stems)
3 onions, one stuck with cloves
3 carrots
3 garlic cloves
A few green celery leaves
4—5 ripe tomatoes or a 1 lb tin, peeled and crushed to pulp
A few spoonfuls of melted lard—goose fat is superior in flavour.
A handful of home-made breadcrumbs (optional)
Salt and pepper, to taste

The beans can be bought in a good delicatessen and are probably
grown in South America where they came from centuries ago.
Pale green flageolets are more expensive but delicate and
quicker and easier to cook.

Wash the beans very carefully, remove suspicious looking
ones. Soak for 2 to 3 hours, no more, said the prudent older
generation, to avoid fermentation in a warm kitchen. Put the
beans in a pan, cover generously with cold, soft water. Bring
to the boil, add the bouquet garni, the vegetables, the pork rind
and salt pork. Cook for 90 minutes; 2 hours if the beans are
hard, it depends on the quality and age. Make quite sure they
do not become mushy.

Meanwhile roast the pork separately in the melted lard or
goose fat. Towards the end of the cooking time for the beans
remove the fresh vegetables and add the garlic sausage, confit
and the roast pork. Cook gently for an extra 30 minutes.

At this stage grill or fry the sausages and add them to the
Cassoulet. Alternatively grill at the last minute and serve with
the Cassoulet on their own.

Cook the Cassoulet in a deep oven dish (earthenware is good
and traditional; it gave its name to the Cassoulet—*une Cassole.*)
Cover the bottom with half the beans, then add the meats cut
into portions and finally the rest of the beans. Add some hot
liquid (water if necessary) and adjust the seasoning—it must
be well flavoured.

Sprinkle the dish with home-made breadcrumbs and dribble
over a little melted lard or goose fat. This last operation gives
a crusty top, but more calories I fear. The early recipes specified
that the crust should be broken and pushed down with a spoon
until a new crust formed, and thus seven times. I do without
this ritual altogether. Sprinkle with plenty of chopped parsley
before serving. 90 minutes to 2 hours of slow baking is necessary
for the blending of all the flavours and to achieve the right texture; and may you then discover 'the amber tone, so special
and characteristic of the flesh in the paintings of Venetian mas-
ters'. This is how Anatole France wrote about the Cassoulet
he enjoyed in a Paris restaurant. Clémence, the cook, officiated
there with continuous dedication and love. After such efforts,
the evening should go well. Fanatics of *nouvelle cuisine*, or the
figure conscious will come another time.

A few decades ago, the baking of the dish took place in the
baker's oven—the perfect method (and possibly the only reli-
BAECKAFFE able oven in the village). It is a practically lost tradition. *Baeckaffe*, a tasty stew from Alsace (lamb, pork and beef with white
wine, potatoes and onions), as the name implies, has to be
cooked in a baker's oven.

Beetroots in my childhood were wrinkled, black and ugly,
but ever so sweet and juicy, and full of flavour. They were
cooked in the baker's oven too (once the bread was removed).
At home they bake well up to 2 hours at 170C/325F/mark 3 and
BEETROOT make simple, rustic refreshing salads with a vinaigrette, chop-
SALAD ped parsley, pepper (it enhances the sweetness), with or without
a touch of garlic. Lamb's lettuce goes well with it, and the colour
contrast is good; crisp chicory blends well too. Mix the salad
just before serving.

Some early memories of childhood remain vivid for ever.
Holding on to my mother's hand, I remember seeing a woman
come out of the bakery, *le fournil*, cross the street and disappear
into the house opposite. She was carrying a large dish with a
roast on it—Sunday lunch, cooked to perfection, courtesy of
the baker. The drifting, tantalising smells must have driven the
dogs of the neighbourhood mad with frustration. I like going
through little French towns, or villages, at lunch time on warm
days. Windows are wide open, cooking smells drift down the

street, never aggressive or unpleasant. At times it almost feels
like an invitation.

CONFIT DE PORC
Pork preserve and how to use it

This preserve can also be used for meats such as duck, goose
and sausages. Maturing in the jar for one month or so improves
the flavour. Whenever you want to use some of the preserve,
remove with a clean fork, always making sure the rest of the
meat is well insulated with lard. Remove the fat from the pieces
of meat by warming gently under the grill or in the oven. There
are many tasty combinations: cold, sliced and eaten simply with
a green salad, or heated through. It is delicious served with sauté
potatoes (using melted lard), a sprinking of finely chopped
parsley and possibly some garlic. A sprig of rosemary added
towards the end of the cooking imparts a very aromatic flavour
(omit the parsley then). It is especially good if the potatoes are
sliced finely and fried in lard. The outside must be golden and
crisp, the inside soft and melting.

Make individual portions with coarsely grated potatoes,
seasoned and bound with a little egg. To keep their lovely tex- PAILLASSONS
ture, these must be eaten as soon as ready. They are known
as *criques* down south—or *paillassons* in Lyon. I think they are
delicious, too, served with a roast.

Poule au Pot

POULE AU POT D'HENRI IV
for Vi's grandson

It was a wonderful surprise to find at home, among the old books—and in French—*Les Mémoires de Sully*, a fascinating story by the adviser, friend and confidant of Henri IV of France. The era was full of passion and intrigue. Elizabeth I was the English monarch; the Stuarts ruled in tumultuous Scotland. With Sully's efforts and innovations and Henri's approval, prosperity reigned in France for a time. Henri, King of Navarre, later of France, spent a lively childhood in and around Pau, the capital. Popular tradition shows him playing with the local boys of his age, heartily and vigorously. Throughout his life he showed sympathy and care for ordinary people. He referred to them as *son bon peuple*, his good people. In turn, they called him *le bon Roi Henri*. He wished his *bon peuple* could afford to eat meat once a week and at least cook a fowl every Sunday— *mettre la poule au pot*—the pot where the usual vegetables, carrots, onions, turnips and leeks were cooking.

Poule au pot really is a complete meal in itself: clear broth, meats in abundance, a choice of vegetables, dumpling, stuffing, not to mention all the left-overs for the next day, and maybe the day after!

The fowl—never a chicken—gives plenty of flavour to the stock. The meat in the lengthy, gentle bubbling comes out beautifully tender—a whole meal, succulent and plentiful. After a year or two of laying, the hen is no longer economical to feed and it ends in the cooking pot.

For country people farming is close to the realities of life, the economy of survival cannot afford to indulge in over-sentimentality. Farming has changed, sometimes for the better, though not always. Because I wanted fresh free-range eggs and since I lived in the country, the simplest way was to keep hens. Bruised corn was their main diet. The rewards came fast and regularly, day after day. My husband called my hens *egg chutes*. Visions of *Poule au pot*, vaguely, but surely, loomed in the distance. When the time came I had a closer look. These hens,

hybrid breeds, were engineered purely to lay eggs. Sadly, they
would never get plump—egg-chutes indeed, but little else. As
I was discussing this dilemma, a friend suggested her line of
action, 'Mince them!' How could I possibly do it? I sold them
eventually, a non-commital and possibly cowardly solution.
Maybe I felt it was more befitting or honourable to end in tasty
stock, with a tasty stuffing. I came across an appropriate com-
ment in Meg Dod's cookery book (1806). There is an anecdote
about a *grand gourmand*, a man of *ultra goût*, who soaked his
Westphalia hams in Rhine wine and baked them in French wine
with aromatic spices. 'It was a fine thing to be a pig in them
days'.

The *poule au pot* varies from one region to the other, from
one family to the next, according to local resources, and eventually each recipe becomes a cook's special recipe. One thing, however, is indisputable. This dish is worthless without a good old
fashioned layer, free-range, naturally, and fed on grain. Following the hows and whys of old or well established recipes can
be most interesting. Meat was expensive and not plentiful and
it had to feed as many people as possible. A filling was the ideal
solution. The fowl, once cleaned, offered the solution. Bread
is the bulk ingredient for the stuffing (stale bread preferably),
the chopped liver and heart add plenty of flavour and herbs from
the garden: chives, tarragon and parsley. Garlic, especially in
the south, gives the distinctive and essential touch.

King Henri loved garlic from birth. His grandfather, then
King of Navarre, gave him a special welcome into the world.
He rubbed his lips with a clove of garlic and gave him a taste
of *jurançon* (the local Pyrennean white wine). Every French
child knows, or knew, the story! A symbolic gesture to help
forge a strong nature and character, essential for survival in
those days. His love for the pungent flavour never stopped. Even
(and especially) his mistresses complained about it. A sprig of
parsley or spearmint, or a pill box filled with peppercorns to
crunch might have sweetened his breath. Coffee beans or
chlorophyll I would suggest nowadays, or abstinence!

I used to watch fascinated as my mother prepared the *poule au
pot*. I learnt a lot as she went along, stopping on the way to
point out the different parts of the bird. The gall bladder had

to be removed from the liver very, very carefully; if it burst, the liver became bitter and inedible. These sessions helped to develop my curiosity; it was like detective work! The gizzard, once opened, showed gravel, grain or grass eaten on that day. Sometimes there was a treasure inside the fowl—golden eggs—a string of yolks dwindling in size (eggs in the making); my mother would say, with a tinge of respect, 'a good layer'. These yolks coloured and bound the stuffing beautifully. A good seasoning was added and the stuffing was ready. It was spooned into the bird; one or two stitches with kitchen thread secured the stuffing before the fowl went into the simmering stock. It was well flavoured with vegetables, giblets from the hen: neck, gizzard, feet (blanched and pared, as always nothing was wasted), a bone, probably salt pork in those days, and occasionally a little raw ham, *jambon de campagne*, especially in Navarre. Later, with the changes in agriculture and economy, a piece of boiling beef would boost the flavour further.

POULE AU POT
The traditional recipe

First, a large pot holding up to 4 litres/7 pints water, though
   3 litres/5 pints might just do.
1 free-range hen of up to 3 kg/6 lb
$\frac{1}{2}$ kg/1 lb carrots
3 onions, with a clove stuck in one of them
2—3 leeks
2 small turnips or parsnips
2—3 celery stalks or a piece of celeriac
3 cloves of garlic
Bouquet garni (bay leaf, parsley, thyme)
Ham bone (with a little meat on it)
250 g/$\frac{1}{2}$ lb lean bacon or boiling beef
Giblets
Extra vegetables (same as above)

Fill the pot with water, add the vegetables, the meat, bones, giblets and salt. Bring to the boil, simmer for one full hour before adding the stuffed fowl. Once the fowl is in the pot, simmer gently for $1\frac{1}{2}$ hours, on average. With the slow simmering the stock should be clear, the hen tasty and tender. Do make 67

sure that it is not overcooked, the exact length of time depends
on the age of the bird, the older the longer! Thirty minutes
or so before the *Poule au pot* is ready you may add the extra
vegetables.

STUFFING

2 eggs
100 g/4 oz stale bread, more or less bread according to the meat
 content.
Small bunch of parsley
2 cloves of garlic
2 livers (if possible)
1 chicken heart (finely chopped)
100 g/¼ lb streaky bacon or ham
Chives or tarragon if available
Salt and pepper

In a bowl mix the breadcrumbs with the eggs, the finely chopped herbs, the chopped meats and seasoning. Make sure the
flavour is *relevée*, i.e. well seasoned. Fill the hen quite tightly
and secure with a few stitches. This is essential.

More stuffing can be prepared to be cooked either in the same
pot beside the hen or separately. Use pure pork sausage meat,
bread, eggs, seasoning and herbs. Wrap inside blanched green
cabbage leaves and tie with kitchen string. A muslin square
holds everything in place for safer cooking and easier handling
out of the pot. It takes 25 to 30 minutes to cook. This stuffing
is known (with a little imagination) as a *green hen*. A *black hen*
had its stuffings made with the same ingredients plus the blood;
a recipe that belongs almost to the past and rural France with
free-range hens in the poultry yard.

MIQUE
Dumpling

Stock (enough to cover the dumpling)
250 g/½ lb stale bread (soaked briefly in water and squeezed)
3 eggs

Seasoning for a good flavour
150 g/5 oz back fat (from an Italian delicatessen) or very finely
   chopped streaky bacon. I tried once with back fat from the
   butcher. It improves with salting for 24 hours
A little flour

Mix the ingredients together thoroughly: make into a ball, roll
in flour and cook in some stock for 30 minutes. I have come
across a similar recipe in old English cooking, but usually the
dumpling is made into smaller individual ones. There are no
potatoes in the traditional recipe. They became acceptable in
Europe well after their discovery in America. In France, in the
18th century, Parmentier eventually made them popular. Any
recipe with Parmentier implies potatoes, like *Potage Parmentier*,
or *Hachis Parmentier* (a type of cottage-pie). If potatoes are HACHIS
required, cook separately, otherwise the stock will become PARMENTIER
cloudy. A large dumpling replaces potatoes and bread anyway.
There are variations in the recipe. This simple version from
the Dordogne area made with bread and is called a *mique* (the
name once given to bread, or a loaf of bread, in the south west).
Like any dumpling, it is fun, symbolic of the past and of that
area. All the same, it is optional.

Serve the broth from the pot on its own to start the meal or
with vermicelli. A little saffron improves the colour and the
flavour, probably a legacy of the Arab influence when they were
in the south. My mother used to colour *bouillon* (broth) with BOUILLON
a little dark caramel. It is quick and easy.
   I must mention a custom, once popular in the country, which
may be manly or hearty, but not for me. When the soup bowls
are almost empty, red wine from the bottle can be added to
them. This is called a *faire chabrot*. It is cooling but I don't FAIRE CHABROT
think it improves the wine or the bouillon . . .
   The fowl may be served in very a large dish (the Scottish
ashet/assiette) surrounded with the vegetables and sliced stuffing. The dumpling is shared around. Mustards and pickles are
excellent and in keeping, or else a piquant sauce with chopped
egg, oil, parsley, pickled gherkins and a shallot, finely chopped.
   All these explanations may seem quite lengthy, but it does
not take long with a little organisation (vegetables prepared
ahead, stuffings and fowl ready in advance), only the cooking 69

time cannot be curtailed. To close the section on the traditional recipe, when *Poule au pot* appeared week after week in country kitchens, this is what an inventive mother would sometimes do: if the fowl is tender (which will be the case after gentle poaching) place it in a separate pan for a few minutes in a hot oven to colour on all sides. It is more appealing for children. *Poule au pot* turned into roast chicken, with roast potatoes (first cooked separately in some stock).

POULET FARCI
Poached Chicken

Here are variations for a sort of *Poule au pot* for those who cannot acquire the right type of free-range hen. I hope this will not raise too many eyebrows from purists! Make a good flavoured stock, and in it poach a young plump chicken, fed on grain preferably. It is better than what is known in France as *le poulet industriel*. The difference between the recipes is essentially in the making of the stock. It must boost the flavour of the chicken.

The first time I tried this recipe, I boosted the stock with an old pheasant. A mature pigeon makes an excellent stock and is neither too expensive nor 'gamey'. Add giblets, a good ½ kg/ 1 lb, coloured beforehand in a little fat or oil to make them more tasty and impart more flavour. There are many ways of making a good stock; a little boiling beef goes with it naturally, as in the previous recipe. A small handful of dried wild mushrooms adds a lively flavour and colour, be they cèpes, chanterelles or ordinary field mushrooms.

The dish is slightly different from the original recipe, more sophisticated. It is worth making for 8 people at least. Left-overs can be used later in several tasty ways, at little cost and little extra work.

INGREDIENTS FOR STOCK

Meats and bones
1 onion with clove
3 carrots
½ a turnip
2 leeks (green included)

2—3 celery stalks with leaves
Lovage, if available
Bouquet garni
Water

Bring all these ingredients to the boil and cook gently for 1 to
1½ hours. Skim whenever necessary. Make the same stuffing
as previously, or for a richer one, use less bread and more meat
(minced and seasoned pork, herbs, chopped ham or veal, for
example). The stuffed chicken is then poached in the well-
flavoured broth. About 20 minutes before the dish is cooked
add the fresh vegetables, the previous ones having given their
best to the stock. Here is a selection to choose from: a small
celeriac, carrots, leeks, a few parsnips or beet ribs tied in bundles
(500—700 g/1—1½ lbs), fennel. In season, a few French beans
or a few mangetout peas cooked in such a tasty stock can only
do well. Do not overcook, but make sure they are tender all
the same. A selection of three or four will do.

A dumpling remains very much an option. The previous
recipe can be made more sophisticated with small dumplings
poached separately for a few minutes in clear stock and served
with it at the beginning of the meal.

SMALL DUMPLINGS WITH HERBS

As in the Mique, prepare fine breadcrumbs, add finely chopped
herbs (tarragon, parsley, chives), bind with eggs and a little thick
cream (instead of finely chopped back fat), season well, work
together and make into small balls. Roll in flour. Poach in the
stock just before serving.

When the dish is ready and the chicken is nicely cooked, pour
out enough stock for the soup. Sieve carefully, remove any fat
with kitchen paper and check the seasoning. If the stock is not
strong enough, concentrate the flavour with extra boiling and
add a little dry sherry or port before serving.

On a plate arrange the carved bird and the stuffing, made
as in the traditional recipe or to your own taste; serve the vegetables separately. The tender bird deserves a delicate sauce;
light, creamy and flavoured with lemon juice and grated lemon
rind.

71

LEMON SAUCE

3 large egg yolks
½ litre/1 pint consommé
250 ml/½ pint cream
Juice of 2 lemons with the grated rind
1 dsp arrowroot or cornflour

In the pan mix the yolks, the cream, the grated rind, the diluted
arrowroot and lemon juice. Add the consommé slowly, stirring
all the time. Cook on a low heat very briefly until the sauce
thickens. Season to taste. Serve in a sauce bowl.

COLD POACHED CHICKEN

If the dish is to be eaten cold, it takes on a completely different
character. It is worth trying. The consommé is reheated before
the meal. The stuffing is served cold and sliced like a terrine
with a little salad on each plate, a colourful and tasty mixture;
select from radicchio, endive, spinach, chicory, corn salad,
watercress, a few leaves of land cress (more pungent), dandelion,
sliced radishes, etc. Serve with a light vinaigrette flavoured with
walnut.

Walnut oil is delicious and fruity, but not always available;
besides it does not keep long. I make do with finely crushed
walnuts (100 g/4 oz) mixed with oil; add salt. It is covered for
a few days, the flavour is delicious. Keep what is left in the
fridge.

After the little salad, serve the meats and vegetables as a
fondue méridionale with an anchoïade sauce. This is a sauce made
with puréed anchovies, olive oil and crushed garlic, and a little
butter (omitted in the traditional anchoïade). I use it for extra
aroma. Cooked on a slow heat it is most aromatic and almost
irresistible—just like snail butter, which has made snails so popular in Britain. In 1773 Samuel Johnson would not have thought
it was possible. In his *Journey to the Western Islands of Scotland*
he wrote confidently, 'an Englishman is not easily persuaded
to dine on snails with an Italian, on frogs with a Frenchman,
on horseflesh with a Tartar'. Two centuries later he would have
72 to rephrase the sentence, on account of snails and frogs. As for

horses, nothing has changed, or will change, I hope.

Keep the *anchoïade* hot and use it as a tasty dip. It has the informality of a fondue, *en famille* or with friends and is always a great success. Each guest helps himself to meat (cut and sliced beforehand) and to tender vegetables.

Hot or cold, traditional or not so traditional, with this recipe a plump chicken becomes different and more interesting. A well established recipe can sometimes be modified, transformed to suit changes, and keep its appeal and quality. The choice of chicken is very important. If the cook (the customer) is determined, eventually the shopkeeper will provide what she needs; after all, he needs her custom too!

VARIOUS WAYS TO SERVE THE STOCK

The stock, simply reheated and well seasoned becomes a fine soup flavoured with a little port. This was considered a good reviver for convalescents. Honeymoon couples benefitted from it too; some of their 'considerate friends', having discovered their hide-out, would bring them early in the morning some consommé laced with port, sprinkled generously with pepper to renew their ardour—happy couple!

Add finely sliced savoury herb pancakes (parsley, tarragon, chervil) to each bowl or plate. The pancakes can be prepared ahead.

A simple liaison with cream, yolk, lemon juice, added to the hot stock before serving, gives colour and smoothness with a lemony tang. Sprinkle with chervil or parsley.

With the left-over chicken stock make an extra special cream of vegetable soup with fennel, lettuce, or nettles in spring—the vegetable of your choice.

A little chicken meat (off the bone) finely sliced can be added to the hot stock with freshly chopped mint and chives. Some of the meat (pheasant, boiled beef, etc) used to flavour the stock, minced and mixed with some herbs and egg, can be turned into mini-balls for a more substantial soup.

73

IDEAS FOR LEFT-OVER MEAT

The meat used to flavour the stock, minced and seasoned with chopped and fried onions can be turned into a cottage pie similar to *Hachis Parmentier* (i.e. mince with layers of puréed potatoes and a sprinkling of gruyère cheese).

HACHIS
PARMENTIER

A *Hachis Parmentier* is usually made the day after a *pot au feu* (boiled beef). Special cuts of boiling beef are boiled in the pot with the usual vegetables. A good marrow bone should always be included.

CHICKEN
GRATINÉE

Chicken gratinée served with rice is easy to put together. Mix the cooked chicken pieces, or slices, with a sauce made with stock, cornflour, tarragon and a little cream. Grated cheese (Gruyère, Gouda, Emmenthal) sprinkled in between layers makes it tastier. Home-made breadcrumbs sprinkled on top, dotted with butter, give it a crunchy topping after 30 minutes or so in the oven. Do not add salt; the cheese and consommé have plenty. If there is barely enough meat left, add 250 gm/ $\frac{1}{2}$ lb sliced mushrooms sautéed in a little butter and lemon juice. There will be plenty for all.

BALLOTINE DE POULET
Boned Chicken

In Meg Dod's cookery book there is a recipe to *farce* a fowl '*a favourite old fashioned English dish*'. In fact it is a *ballotine*, much more lengthy to prepare, as the fowl is boned entirely and filled with the stuffing before being poached in good stock — a stock using practically the same vegetables as in a *poule au pot*. Here is a modified version. It can of course be used as a stuffing for the *poule au pot*.

STUFFING FOR A BALLOTINE

125 g/4$\frac{1}{2}$ oz minced ham
125 g/4$\frac{1}{2}$ oz minced veal
100 g/4 oz minced streaky bacon or pork sausage meat
1 chopped onion
1 tbsp chopped herbs (parsley, tarragon or chervil)
2 chopped hard boiled yolks (optional)

1 tsp grated lemon peel (adds a lovely tang)
Cayenne
Salt and Pepper
2 eggs for binding

Mix all the ingredients thoroughly and pack it into the boned chicken. Stitch it up well before poaching in the stock. The fowl is served with a sauce made from the stock, thickened with *beurre manié*. Take off the heat and serve straightaway.

In Dordogne, in a good traditional hotel, I chose chicken terrine on the menu. It was extremely tasty and light, made simply with slices of *Poule au pot*, pieces of rich stuffing (no bread in it), held with an excellent, well-flavoured jellied consommé, a sophisticated version of *poule au pot*. The cooking in this case does not require a large pot, just enough well-flavoured stock to poach the chicken in, with a calf's foot or pig's trotter to make the jelly. Aspic jelly is easier. Whichever method is chosen, boil the stock beforehand to concentrate it.

The terrine was served with cherries pickled in vinegar and lightly whipped cream flavoured with chopped tarragon and grated lemon rind—an original, attractive accompaniment.

CÈRISES AU VINAIGRE
Pickled cherries

1 kg/2 lb firm ripe cherries
½ litre/1 pint wine vinegar, or enough to cover the fruit
150 g/5 oz sugar
1 or 2 cloves (optional)
A few coriander seeds (optional)

Cut a little off the stalks. Arrange in a glass jar. Warm the vinegar to melt the sugar, pour over the cherries and spices (optional). Keep for two months before using. Grapes can be prepared the same way.

Poissons

POISSONS
Fish

When I first arrived in Britain, wild salmon and trout were the fish I enjoyed the most. Everything else was sold filleted and the choice in small towns or in the country was limited. According to the fishmonger, the fault lay with the housewife and her lack of adventure. Whenever he tried a new line he was left with unsold fish and was out of pocket. This was two or three decades ago, and on both sides everybody is more adventurous now.

It is not so very long ago that there was a glut of salmon in Scotland: what is called nowadays *saumon sauvage* or wild salmon. As I chatted with a Frenchman in Scotland on a fishing expedition, I learnt of the much lamented disappearence of salmon in the Dordogne river. It starts like a fabulous story. Once, three times a year when the salmon came back up to their breeding grounds, the town crier summoned villagers with a roll on his drum. 'Oyez, oyez, hurry, gather your nets, the salmon are back.' Men and women rushed down the river. As the men netted the fish, the women gathered them in huge bags. Some would be eaten fresh, poached or grilled, or else sliced and fried. To keep a more lasting supply some were cured by smoking in the wide fireplaces usual in those days in rural France. This ingenious way of keeping fish or meat imparts new flavours. Such processes as smoking and salting, developed along the generations through necessity and observation, follow the progress of man, although, in the last decades, short cuts used to salt or smoke food gain time at the expense of quality.

In those areas blessed once with miraculous catches but no refrigeration, salmon was at times too much of a good thing. Hired labourers, on both sides of the Channel, demanded that salmon should be eaten no more than three times a week! This glut is no longer a problem. Recipes that use small amounts of salmon are welcome.

KEDGEREE AU SAUMON
Salmon Kedgeree

This traditional English recipe with an Indian flavour is an 79 excellent example of how to have an elegant main dish with a small amount of salmon. I omit the curry and use herbs or saffron. Among the herbs, parsley is excellent: plenty, finely chopped, as the traditional recipe requires. It can be mixed with chives, chervil, dill or tarragon. These blend successfully with salmon. Hardboil 4 eggs and chop them coarsely. A piece of left-over salmon is ideal for a kedgeree. (If it is not available, COURT BOUILLON buy a fresh cut—one pound—and cook it in a simple *court bouillon*, flavoured with lemon and white wine and salt). It can be used afterwards to impart extra flavour to the Italian rice. I enjoy its flavour and texture and it stays moist, strands of saffron add colour and yet more flavour—saffron combines well with fish and rice. Any favourite recipe for kedgeree can be adapted to these suggestions. It is a perfect dish, provided it is served as soon as it is ready.

Flake the salmon, add to the hot rice with butter, cream, herbs and eggs at the last minute. If the dish should wait make sure it does not dry out and that it is covered.

To the suggestions mentioned before, you could add to your salmon kedgeree cheaper cuts of smoked salmon (if they have been frozen make sure they are not too salty). If salmon has been for too long in the deep freeze it may get rather salty.

I enjoy potted shrimps mixed with the hot kedgeree—only a small quantity is required. It will give a lift to an ordinary kedgeree with its spicy and buttery flavour. Potted shrimps was one of my favourite starters when I came to Britain. Nowadays, if bought deep-frozen, I find them salty and on the dry side.

RILLETTES AUX DEUX SAUMONS
Potted Salmon

This has the same creamy and rich texture as the more traditional *pork rillettes*, but is quite a different recipe. It is easy, quick and adaptable.

For 6 people
Court-bouillon
   1 pint white wine and water in equal parts
   Peel of 1 lemon, sliced
   Salt
500 g/1 lb salmon

225 g/½ lb smoked salmon trimmings
1 small jar of red salmon eggs
150 g/5 oz butter softened
1 tbsp cream
Juice and grated rind of 1 lemon, previously scrubbed or wiped
    with vinegar
1 large yolk
A little dill
Salt and pepper

Poach the salmon in the *court-bouillon* for 10 minutes at the
most. Leave in the liquid and cool. Flake and mix with half
the smoked salmon, the egg yolk, lemon juice, grated peel and
dill. Blend until smooth with the butter. Add the rest of the
smoked salmon, chopped coarsely, the salmon eggs and a couple
of spoonfuls of *court-bouillon*, concentrated by more cooking
with bones and skin. Check before seasoning as the smoked
salmon may be rather salty. Put in an elegant bowl and cool
for a few hours to let the flavours develop.

To look like the traditional *rillettes*, cover with a layer of
melted butter sharpened with a grated lemon rind and juice.
It is simple but festive.

SAUMON KOULIBIAC
Salmon Pie

Koulibiac or Coulibiac, is German in its early and humble
origin: a pie in which the main ingredient was cabbage plus
fish and *vesiga*, dried off spine marrow from the sturgeon.
Known mainly as a Russian dish, it is now more sophisticated.
It is encased in a brioche dough (the bread dough of early days
has been replaced by it, enriched with eggs, butter and milk).
The Salmon Koulibiac I know is much simplified and is made
with puff-pastry (bought good quality puff-pastry is excellent
and simplifies the work.)

For 6 to 8 people
600—700 g/1½ lb salmon
100 g/4 oz long grain rice (Italian is my favourite for this recipe,
    yet again.)
500 g/1 lb puff pastry (roll the ready made puff-pastry more
    thinly)

350 g/¾ lb mushrooms
3 hard boiled eggs
75 g/3 oz butter
300 ml/10 fl.oz cream
Bunch of chives and parsley
Salt and pepper

Cook the rice and lay to one side. Left-over salmon can be used, otherwise cook the salmon in a *court-bouillon* (quickly prepared with water and white wine, in equal parts) with lemon slices, fish bones, if available, and sea salt. This *court-bouillon* can be used straight away. Add fish, bring slowly to the boil, simmer for a few minutes, take off the heat but leave the fish in the liquid (stock) until cold. It will be nicely flavoured and of perfect consistency. Roll out the pastry about ½ cm/¼ inch thick and spread half of it in the bottom of a rectangular baking dish. Spread with a layer of rice, the chopped eggs mixed with finely chopped mushrooms softened in a little butter and the cream mixed with the herbs, always leaving space all round the filling so the layers of pastry can be joined . Add the flaked salmon and finally the rest of the rice. Wrap with the rest of the pastry— moisten the edges with water or egg wash to join the layers of pastry together and seal the pie well. Decorate (optional) with left-over pastry leaves; crescents, fish scales etc. Brush all over with egg wash for colour and an attractive appearance.

SAUCES

The traditional sauce is made with melted butter and lemon juice with the grated rind for good measure, served in a sauce bowl—make plenty.

Make a delicate, light, white sauce with a little cornflower mixed with some *court-bouillon* and enriched with a little cream to which is added a jar of smoked salmon or prawn butter.

SAUMON TARTARE
Salmon Tartare

As with *steak tartare* freshness is paramount, but the sauce for the fish must be lighter and more subtle. The gherkins should

be large and mildly pickled in dill. For 1 lb of fillets make a
mayonnaise with 1 yolk.

For 6 people
500 g/1 lb fresh uncooked wild salmon
300 ml vegetable oil
1 yolk
2 large gherkins, chopped and drained
1 tsp finely chopped dill or mint
1 tsp finely chopped chives
1 small jar salmon eggs
3 lemons or limes
6 lemon quarters
Sea salt and pepper
Make a mayonnaise with the yolk and oil. Chop the salmon very
finely and marinate in the lemon or lime juice and a spoonful
of oil for one hour or so. Pour off the excess juice and mix well
with the gherkins, herbs, salt and freshly ground black pepper.
Mix with the mayonnaise. Once the *tartare de saumon* is ready,
divide among the plates, and decorate with lemon quarters, dill
or mint and salmon eggs.

In France the *tartare* I tried was served with chips! I prefer
fine slices of brown bread and lemon butter (add the finely
grated rind of one of the lemons to some creamed butter). Other
options include a light green salad flavoured with cream (or
walnut oil), lemon juice and pepper, or else a cucumber garnish,
English style. *Monkfish Tartare* is another alternative, without
mayonnaise but with a *coulis de tomate* (fresh tomato pulp,
puréed, seasoned, flavoured with chervil or lemon).

TRUITE AUX AMANDES
Trout with Almonds

The very first trout I ate came from a Pyrenean mountain
stream; the wild brown trout I had in Scotland were caught
in local rivers. My favourite recipe has always been *truite aux
amandes*; it is easy and tasty.

For 4 people
1 trout per person

50 g/ 2 oz butter
2 tbsp oil
2 lemons
1 glass (15 cl/5 fl.oz) dry white wine
75 g/3 oz sliced almonds

Bake the almonds in the oven or toast under the grill until coloured and crisp. (Be careful, they turn brown and bitter very quickly). Gut the trout, rinse in cold water and dry with kitchen paper. Roll in flour and fry in a large frying pan pre-heated with oil and a little of the butter. When nicely coloured on one side, turn over and finish cooking on a reduced heat. It takes about 10 minutes. Do not overcook at the risk of eating dry and tasteless fish. On the other hand, pink and undercooked trout is not right either. (Undercooked fish, like meat, can contain parasites). When ready, arrange on a flat serving dish. Add salt and pepper, the juice of one lemon and keep warm. Pour away the used fat, deglaze the pan with wine and whisk in, off the heat, the rest of the butter cut into two or three pieces. Pour the sauce over the trout and finally scatter it generously with the crunchy almonds. Decorate with lemon quarters or peeled segments of orange or lemon rolled in finely chopped parsley.

Farm trout is cheaper and more plentiful than wild trout. Unfortunately the flavour and the texture can be disappointing. It varies according to the diet and the breeding waters—the cooler the better, closer to the trout's natural habitat.

PINK TROUT
MOUSSE
With pink fillets sold at the fishmonger one can prepare new dishes: light and attractive mousses made with eggs and cream and cooked in a *bain-marie*. Sauces flavoured with tarragon, chervil or basil, will, according to the choice, change the nature of the dish.

Fillets, plain or lightly smoked, cooked briefly in butter decorate most delicately a green salad mixed with citrus fruits (such as watercress and orange).

TROUT
MARINADE
Raw fillets, marinated in lemon juice and grated rind with a little oil make a salad attractive and substantial. For 500 g/1 lb fish use the juice of 3 large lemons. Cut the fillets into strips and add to the salad, seasoned with a fruity oil.

HARENGS À LA MOUTARDE
Herrings with Mustard

This recipe is best in winter when herrings are at their peak. The dish with its rich flavour, appreciated on a cold day, does not overload the family budget and it is highly nutritious.

Use boned herrings. Before cooking them, cut one or two slashes across the fish. Coat thickly in mustard or *moutarde forte de Dijon*. (French mustard, by the way, is known as *moutarde douce*.) Dribble a little oil over the fish and cook under a hot grill. Turn over when it is cooked and coloured on one side. It will only take 8 to 10 minutes in all. Finish cooking and enjoy this simple dish, full of flavour. It is not fiery, since mustard loses its pungency as it cooks.

Serve with steamed or boiled potatoes, tossed in butter and sprinkled with parsley. I like plain rice and a mustard-flavoured sauce to go with the fish. Try cream mixed with horse-radish sauce or with a good mustard (it could be green pepper mustard), yoghurt whisked with mustard (less calories), mayonnaise with mustard or simply a creamy white sauce with mustard. These sauces are quick and easy. The last one, the most lengthy, is the most traditional.

Mackerel with mustard is equally good. This is a firm fish which must be enjoyed at the peak of freshness. MACKEREL WITH MUSTARD

MORUE
Salt Cod

Fresh cod, or *cabillaud*, is used differently from salt cod (*la morue*). Cod comes from the cold waters of the North Sea. The surplus was salted by local fishermen and taken down south (Spain, France, Italy). There it was sold in exchange for other goods—a barter.

It became the main source of fish for poorer people and those in areas distant from the coast. Later, fishermen from the Basque areas of France and Spain went to catch the fish as far as Iceland. Small trawlers and rough winter seas turned cod fishing into a gruelling expedition. Popular novels like Loti's *Pêcheurs d'Islande* (Fishermen of Iceland) caught the imagination of the French last century. The novel has now gone more 85 or less into oblivion, but I am almost certain it was the reason why evening prayers with mother never failed to mention 'those poor fishermen on the stormy seas'.

There is less salt cod these days and it is getting rare and expensive—the law of supply and demand. In my schooldays, every Friday was fish day. *Brandade de morue*, a creamy, tasty dish, meant, for us, salt cod boiled and mixed with mashed potatoes. The taste was not particularly appealing and there was always a bone or two lurking in it. The last time I tasted the real thing was in Central Spain. It was light and creamy, served in small portions as a starter with crisp toast and olives—a treat. The recipe was very similar to the Provençal one; poached fish, flaked, mixed slowly (originally it was pounded) with olive oil and hot milk alternatively, until the right consistency was reached. A little garlic can also be pounded into it.

As I was longing for a taste of salt cod in the winter, I experimented with fresh cod. Fresh cod coated all over with coarse sea salt looked within a few hours quite different. It had shrunk and lay in a pool of watery liquid. Two days later I tried the reverse process by soaking the fish in plenty of fresh water, and I made my first version of *brandade* with a mixer, adding, slowly, olive oil and light cream like a mayonnaise. Since I could not compete with the real thing, I simply added some well-creamed potatoes (the same weight as the fish), seasoned to taste, piled in a dish and decorated with black olives and fried croûtons. It was very good.

This is how I deal with nostalgia—the positive way. The salt definitely made the cod more tasty. The mixture could be used for making fishcakes with parsley and garlic, and using saffron or good tumeric to give a sunny colour. A fresh tomato sauce makes it tasty and colourful. Peel some ripe fresh tomatoes, squeezed to get rid of some of the liquid. Purée, or chop finely, and flavour with parsley or basil (to taste) and add a little salt and pepper as required.

POISSON À LA PORTUGAISE
Portuguese Fish

For 4 people

4 cod steaks

2 medium-sized onions, sliced
2 tsp hot paprika (to taste)
3 tbsp olive oil or ground nut oil (*arachide*)
1 large glass dry white wine
350g/¾ lb potatoes finely sliced
Salt and pepper

In a hot oven, heat a large shallow ovenproof dish. Add the oil, the potatoes and lay the fish on top. Add a little salt and pepper. Cover with the sliced onions and the paprika and season again. Add the wine. When it starts cooking reduce the heat and let it simmer gently for 20 minutes or so. My Portuguese friends served this dish with tomatoes cut in half, sprinkled with some freshly chopped basil mixed with breadcrumbs and a little oil, cooked in the oven with the fish or separately.

SOLE AU LAIT
Sole Cooked in Milk

A Portuguese friend gave me this recipe. The flavour is delicate and pleasant and it is easy to make.

Lay fresh fillets of sole in a shallow buttered baking dish, cover with milk and sprinkle with ground home-made bread-crumbs. Dot with butter. Cook in the oven for 20 minutes. The top becomes crusty and the fish creamy. Serve with lemon quarters and steamed potatoes or plain rice.

This is how I make the recipe a little more sophisticated. While the sole is in the oven, fry briefly in a little butter one sliced scallop per person. Lay to one side. Peel and slice some cucumber and fry for a short time in the same pan. These can be served around the edge of the sole.

FILLET DE POISSON
Fried Fish Fillet

Choose medium sized pieces of sole, whiting or haddock (the larger ones are not so easy to handle). Dip the fish in milk, then roll lightly in flour, shaking off the excess. Fry in a large enough frying pan with hot fat to give a crunchy coating. For sole use 87

butter, or butter and oil; for a less delicate fish oil is excellent.
It is easy, quick and much lighter than batter of any kind.

If a slight change is wanted, season the flour with curry
powder and serve the fish with fried bananas and rice—a touch
of the exotic in everyday cooking! With more time to spare,
make banana fritters, to go with the fish.

HARENGS FUMÉS MARINÉS
Marinated Kippers

For 4 to 6 people
4—8 kipper fillets
2 lemons (the juice)
2 tbsp oil
2 or 3 shallots or one onion, finely sliced
Pepper

When the kippers are not so juicy and at their peak, it is better
to marinate them. Buy boned kippers and remove the skin; it
comes off very easily. Cut the fillets in strips, 1.5 cm/$\frac{1}{2}$ inch
wide, and lay in a dish (pyrex or earthenware). Add the lemon
juice and a little of the oil. It not only flavours the fish, but
it softens any bone that might still be in it. Next day add oil,
freshly ground pepper, and shallots or finely sliced onion. Serve
with warm potato salad, or with buttered brown crusty bread
LEMON   or a hot baguette spread with lemon butter (creamed butter with
BUTTER a little grated lemon rind).

PÂTÉ DE MAQUEREAU FUMÉ
Smoked Mackerel Pâté with Avocado

Smoked mackerel makes a delicious fish pâté or spread. Mix
thoroughly the same weight of avocado and smoked mackerel
and add some lemon juice to prevent discolouration. Flavour
with green pepper mustard. It is simple, quick and economical.
If it is not eaten straightaway, cover tightly with clingfilm and
keep in the fridge. In these simple recipes the quantities can
88   be adapted to taste and requirement.

Adapted for different fish in cooler areas

In Corsica, I tasted a wonderful fish soup, all the better since I watched its making from the moment the fish were brought in early one morning. The fishermen willingly answered all my questions about these colourful, recently caught fish. They had different roles. The softer ones would be puréed with the soup, while the others, firmer or larger, would be eaten afterwards with a fragrant *aïoli* (garlic mayonnaise). According to Frédéric Mistral, the Provençal writer, the *aïoli* concentrates 'toute l'allégresse du soleil de Provence'—all the *joie de vivre* of Provençal sunshine.

Away from the Mediterranean and its special varieties of fish, it is still possible to make tasty, appetising, well-flavoured fish soup. Choose different types for a mixture of textures and flavours; small crabs for plenty of taste, monkfish or very fresh mackerel for texture, whiting, for example, to give flavour and body to the soup.

For 6 people

2 kg/4 lb fish (cod, small crabs, whiting, haddock, mackerel, or monkfish, for example)

3 tbsp olive oil

3 cloves garlic

2 onions

1 leek

Saffron, of good quality

Bouquet garni (parsley, or parsley stems, 2 bay leaves, thyme)

Orange rind

Piece of fennel (or 1 tbsp fennel seed)

Parsley and chives, finely chopped

2 tomatoes, large and ripe

2 litres/3½ pints water

Fresh prawns and a few crawfish, unshelled, give the supreme touch of luxury

Salt and pepper (to taste)

Grated Parmesan or Gruyère cheese (optional)

Fry the vegetables, add the flavourings and herbs. When the vegetables are soft, add the fish and then the water. Cook briskly for 15 to 20 minutes. Keep aside some of the firmer fish to eat after the soup. Purée about half of the soup to thicken the stock. Rather than using a mixer I prefer a small *mouli-légumes*. The fine gauge does not let any bones through. Add the prawns and the crawfish (optional) then check the seasoning. The soup must be highly flavoured. Pour into soup plates with thin slices of dried bread in them. Pass round a bowl of Parmesan or Gruyère cheese (optional).

For the next course serve the firm fish with boiled or steamed potatoes and a garlic mayonnaise (*aïoli*) and scatter the parsley and chives over the top.

The easiest way to make an *aïoli* is to crush 3 to 4 garlic cloves and mix with an egg yolk. Add olive oil (it must be olive oil) very slowly to begin with, stirring all the time. When the sauce begins to thicken, the flow can be increased and wine vinegar and a little lemon juice can be added sparingly, to taste. Be prepared to double the quantities since the sauce is addictive.

UNE HISTOIRE POUR LES PÊCHEURS
A Story for Fishermen

My native part of France is not the best for its great variety of fish dishes. It is inland, and even fresh water fish, carp, pike or small fry are now scarce. From Alphonse Daudet, the Provençal writer I borrow this story of *La bouillabaisse du pêcheur* — the fishermen's bouillabaisse. Some critics have muttered that he had written many of his Provençal stories while he lived in Paris. If so, it proves that nostalgia is a stimulating spice. In a chapter called *Paysages Gastronomiques* (Gastronomic Landscapes) Daudet describes a *couscous* made in Algeria, an *aïoli* in Provence, a *polenta* in Corsica and a *fisherman's bouillabaisse* along the Mediterranean coast. If I had to choose the most vivid and evocative way to cook fish ever to come to my attention, the most stimulating to the senses, it would be this last one.

In the midst of winter, this story, vibrant with sunshine, colours and scents, has on occasion filled my eyes with tears. My only experience of fish *al fresco* was in a *calanque* (a mini fjord) near Cassis, eating a fish freshly caught, cooked on the spot, on fir twigs to the song of cicadas and the strong scent of pine needles in the midday sun. Here are Daudet's recollections of his *bouillabaisse*, as translated by my husband.

We were following the coast of Sardinia, headed for the Isle of Madeleine. A morning excursion. The rower's pace was easy, and, leaning over the side, I stared down into the water, limpid as a spring, sunlit to the seabed. Jelly-fish and starfish were spread out amongst the fronds of sea weed. Large lobsters lay motionless and asleep, their long feelers drooping on the fine sandy bottom. All this clearly visible at a depth of eighteen or twenty feet in an unreal quality of aquamarine-like clarity. In the bows of the boat stood a fisherman with a long shaft of split willow in his hands, motioning to the oarsman, *piano...piano*, and, suddenly his rod would thrust upwards with a splendid lobster between its points, waving its claws, its growing fear still clouded by sleepiness. Close by, another sailor cast his line delicately in the boat's wake, drawing in wonderful little fish whose colour as they expired shifted through countless brightly varying hues. Agony viewed through a prism. The fishing completed, we came ashore through the tall grey rocks. The fire was quickly lit, pale in the bright sunlight; never have I tasted anything finer than that lobster bouillabaisse. And, oh, that siesta afterwards on the sand! A sleep lulled by the lapping of the sea where the myriad flashes of the wavelets flitted before my closed eyes.

Viandes et Gibiers

VIANDES ET GIBIERS
Meat and Game

When choosing pheasants, especially for roasting whole, make sure that there are not too many blemishes, in other words, that they are cleanly shot. The best, naturally, are the wild ones, reared by mother hen in the woods and coverts. Fashion and necessity once required game that was well hung—so long, in fact, that it became green or blue, the early stages of putrefaction no less. In French the word *faisandé* epitomised that condition. But times have changed; hanging pheasants or game for weeks is no longer the rule. The present trend is healthier. It depends on the age of the pheasant, the temperature and personal taste of course. It varies from a couple of days to four; just enough to give flavour to the meat and to make it tender.

In the south of France (Quercy), I had a long chat with a good and friendly butcher. He explained that nowadays he no longer chooses the cattle from the farm. He selects and buys carcasses (a very reliable way he assured me), which means that the hanging time, especially in the south, is halved. Once upon a time, without reliable refrigeration, meat had to hang as long as possible (or bearable). Strong wine marinades with herbs and spices helped to keep game, tenderise the old one and make it more palatable and digestible. A few yards away from our old Scottish house, underground, we have one of these relics of the past—an old ice-larder, known as the monk's larder. It is an old masonry vault, well insulated once, with two thick wooden doors (the hinges remain to testify). Rusty hooks to hang the game are still in place. In the built-in recess, the ice or the packed snow was stored. The meats were supposed to last until late spring: stomachs and taste buds of earlier generations were quite different, less delicate, and gout thrived.

FAISAN AVEC CHOUCROUTE
Pheasant and Sauerkraut

This unusual recipe makes one pheasant go further. The sauerkraut is different and lighter than the traditional type.

For 4 to 6 people
1 pheasant
1 kg/2lb jar or tin sauerkraut
4—5 slices smoked bacon, cut a little thick
Good frankfurters (optional)
1 large onion, finely chopped
2 carrots, finely chopped
3—4 tbsp oil
1 large glass of wine
1 small glass of stock or wine
8—10 juniper berries

The sauerkraut bought in a jar is already pre-cooked, but it has to be livened up by some more slow cooking (30 minutes or so) with the onion and carrots, softened in a little fat, a large glass of Riesling-type wine and the juniper berries. Meanwhile roast the pheasant in a casserole dish. Pour on all sides a little oil, cover with a lid and cook gently for 35 to 40 minutes. At this point remove the pheasant and add to the sauerkraut where it will finish cooking. The sauerkraut will benefit from the association, however brief. Deglaze the casserole with a small glass of stock or wine and add this to the sauerkraut. Parboil the bacon and frankfurters, add to the pheasant, taking care not to overcook, as the pheasant would become dry and tough (10 to 15 minutes). Carve and serve in a hot serving dish with the meats nicely arranged on the sauerkraut together with puréed potatoes, French style, i.e. rather creamy in texture.

FAISAN AU CHOU ROUGE AUX MARRONS
Pheasant with Red Cabbage and Chestnuts
For 6 people
2 young pheasants (hens are more tender)
1—1½ kg/2—3 lb red cabbage
225 g/½ lb dried chestnuts
1 carrot
2 onions
A few bay leaves
30 g/1 oz butter for the chestnuts
3 tbsp oil or good lard

3 tbsp wine
1 large glass of cider or ½ of wine and ½ of water

First cook the pheasants in a casserole with a little salt and with oil spooned over them, for around 45 minutes in all. The juices must be pale pink (check with a fine knitting needle—no risk of losing it). Put aside on a separate dish, deglaze the roasting dish with a little water and white wine. Keep warm and add to the carved roast pheasant before serving.

CABBAGE

Prepare the cabbage (removing damaged leaves and core), slice quite finely before parboiling in vinegary water for 5 minutes. Drain. If possible, use a good size, good quality stewing dish for slow cooking, the cast iron type known in France as a *cocotte* is ideal. (A *cocotte-minute* is a pressure cooker). Soften the chopped onion in a little fat, add the cabbage, the liquid, and cook gently for 30 minutes.

Meanwhile prepare the dry chestnuts. Out of season they have more flavour and texture than the tinned ones. Make sure they come from a reliable shop and have not been lying in bags for long. Cook slowly for 30 minutes in double their volume of water with one or two bay leaves. Once the water is absorbed, they caramelise quickly; it is delicious, as long as it is not overdone. Mix with 30 g/1 oz butter, and a sprinkling of freshly ground pepper. Add to the cooked cabbage and serve hot with the carved pheasants. The cabbage, the pheasants and the sweet and buttery flavours combine deliciously. The drumsticks are not easy and no guest should have to struggle with them! Keep them, and the carcasses for a delicious lentil soup.

After cooking the stock, remove the meat from the bones and purée with some cooked lentils. These tasty left-overs help to make *des lendemains qui chantent*—music for the day after a party or a special meal.

A nice addition to the cabbage and pheasant is slices of eating apples cored, peeled or unpeeled, and softened in butter: a teaspoon of sugar at this stage caramelises quickly; it gives a nice finish and flavour. Arrange in a large dish (warmed up beforehand).

97

SALMIS DE FAISAN
Pheasant Casserole

This is more work than simply roasting a pheasant, but the extra effort is well rewarded.

For 4 people
1 tender pheasant
3 shallots
1 small onion
Oil for roasting
1 clove of garlic
Thyme
Bouquet-garni
1 small glass of brandy
150 ml/5 fl.oz red wine
1 croûton per person (triangular or heart-shaped)
1 — 2 pheasant livers (or mix with chicken livers)
Pepper and salt

Roast a young pheasant for 20 to 25 minutes (it must not be completely cooked). Remove the breasts and legs and keep in a warm place covered with foil. Meanwhile, with the wings, heart, bones, neck and skins, cut as small as possible to make a sauce. Fry 2 chopped shallots and the onion in oil and butter with the bones etc. Add the wine, thyme, parsley and clove of garlic, salt and pepper. Cook gently for 30 minutes with a lid on. Add a little stock, or water if necessary. Sieve the sauce and press down the bones and skins to extract all the juices. Fry the livers with a little butter, salt and pepper, and a finely chopped shallot, then pour in the brandy and flambé. Mix this in a liquidiser and add a little of the sauce if the texture is not smooth enough. Check the seasoning and spread over the fried croûtons. Serve the pheasant, coated with the sauce, on an attractive dish with the croûtons laid round the edge.

SELLE DE LIÈVRE À LA CRÈME
Saddle of Hare with Cream

The following recipe comes from an excellent traditional cook: I have sampled a similar dish in Switzerland. There, they used the meat off the bone; it is easier and quicker to cook. The marinated saddle , roasted in the oven and served with the sauce looks more *special*, more elegant.

1 good sized saddle of young hare
2—3 oz butter
Back fat, 10—12 pieces
Mustard, mixed
Simple marinade
   ½ litre/1 pint red wine (dry white wine gives a lighter flavour)
   1 onion or 2 shallots
1 carrot
2 bay leaves
Peppercorns

Marinate the saddle of hare for 24 hours; take out the saddle, wipe with kitchen paper; lard with small strips of back fat and spread thickly all over with mustard. Cook slowly in the oven with a good quantity of butter (to taste). Baste regularly and often. It takes about an hour in a moderate oven.

THE SAUCE

3 shallots
1 tbsp flour
1 tbsp cream
1 small glass of brandy
Liver from the hare
Salt and pepper

Slice the shallots finely, soften in a pan with a little fat, sprinkle with flour and stir. Cook for a few minutes, then add the cream, the puréed liver and the brandy (optional). Serve the hare with chestnut purée and tartlets filled with cranberries or redcurrants. A green lentil purée with cream is another suggestion.

GIBELOTTE
Wild Rabbit Stew

This is an old fashioned dish made with wild rabbit, *lapin de garenne*, flavoured with herbs and wild mushrooms, (field mushrooms, blewits in the autumn, or chanterelles). Chan-

terelles have a great advantage over other varieties—no worms.
Did nature provide them with a defensive flavour or scent?

Gibelotte is a tasty, simple but substantial country dish prepared nowadays during the shooting season. I have sampled it several times in small, good village restaurants.

For 5 to 6 people
1 wild rabbit (1½—2kg/3—4lb)
3—4 cloves of garlic
Thyme, parsley, marjoram
1 dsp flour (25 g/1 oz)
3 tbsp oil or lard
1 tsp mustard (optional)
½ bottle dry white wine
½ pint stock or water
150 g/5 oz smoked streaky bacon, cut thick
500 g/1 lb onions—the smaller the better for presentation
250 g/½ lb mushrooms

Cut the bacon into cubes and sauté in a deep pan. In France it is usually parboiled beforehand. Joint the rabbit. Remove the bacon from the pan and fry the rabbit in the same fat. When coloured on all sides, sprinkle with flour, stir and cook for a minute or two, then pour in the white wine, add the herbs, garlic and cooked bacon. Then add the stock or water and the small onions and the mushrooms (sautéed beforehand). Cook slowly (with a lid on) for 40 to 45 minutes. Check the seasoning. Serve hot with triangles of fried croûtons and plain potatoes. To give extra flavour to the stew, add mustard when the onions start cooking.

POULET AU VIN BLANC
Chicken in White Wine

A good home-grown chicken will make a far better dish than a bland, cheap, deep-frozen, intensive-farmed supermarket chicken. If it is not free-range, make sure it has been fed on grain.

For 4 people
1 chicken (1½ kg/3½ lb)

3 tbsp oil and butter
4 small carrots
2 onions
200 g/7 oz streaky bacon, smoked and cut thick
½ bottle white wine
1 glass chicken stock
Bouquet-garni (thyme, bayleaf, parsley)
250 g/½ lb chanterelles or cèpes in season
or a tin of champignons de Paris
Seasoning
4 heart-shaped croûtons, fried in oil and garlic
Parsley or chervil

Joint the chicken into 8 pieces and sauté all over in a casserole dish. Add onions, chopped bacon and carrots. When the chicken is getting lightly coloured add the wine. Bring to a brisk boil. Pour in the stock, flavour with the bouquet-garni and season. Cook gently for half an hour. Five minutes before the dish is ready, sauté the mushrooms whole or sliced according to size and add to the chicken. Serve with the croûtons and a sprinkling of finely chopped parsley or chervil. If the sauce is too liquid add, in small pieces, a *beurre manié* (flour and butter blended into a smooth paste).

ALICOT
Giblet Casserole

At Christmas time make a tasty and economical dish with the giblets from turkeys. They are easy to get from a merchant selling fresh birds. This was made at home, too, with giblets from ducks. I remember how good it was.

For 4 people
Giblets from 2—3 birds (necks, wing tips, hearts, gizzards)
4 thickish slices of bacon
5 small onions
1 tbsp flour
4 small carrots
4 small white turnips
2 glasses of chicken stock

1 glass of white wine
1 bouquet-garni
75 g/3 oz green olives, blanched beforehand
Pepper and salt
Parsley

Use a casserole dish. Sauté the giblets and the chopped bacon
in a little oil with one sliced onion. Let it colour, then sprinkle
with the flour. Stir with a wooden spoon for a couple of minutes,
then pour in the stock with the wine. Flavour with the herbs.
Let it simmer for 20 minutes or so. At this point slice the carrots
and the turnips and add them to the casserole with the olives
and onions. Season to taste. After half an hour of gentle cooking
the dish is ready. For a more substantial recipe add some small
potatoes to the casserole 20 minutes before the end. Serve with
a good sprinkling of chopped parsley.

CUISSES DE CANARD
Duck Legs

Nowadays it is easy to find duck legs sold on their own while
the breast, meatier and leaner, is sold separately at a much
higher price. What to do with duck legs? The dish described
here was sampled in Provence in a small restaurant. With cold,
grilled peppers, sliced and seasoned with vinaigrette, followed
by a light raspberry tart, it made a simple, tasty and cheap meal.

For 4 people
1 or 2 legs per person
75 g/3 oz small green olives
75 g/3 oz black olives
1 head of garlic, left unpeeled
Thyme, to taste
Salt and pepper
1 glass water or stock or half water and wine

If green olives are too bitter or too salty for your liking, blanch
them for a minute or so. Cook the duck legs in a little fat on
a medium heat for 5 minutes. The meat will render fat. Drain
it after frying if you want a light lean dish. Start the cooking
all over again with a spoonful of oil. Add the olives, the garlic,

the thyme and seasoning. When the cooking has started, add the water or stock (or half wine and water). Cook until the sauce has reduced and is getting thicker. Serve with sautéed potatoes and the traditional green salad.

My mother used to make duck casserole with white wine, bitter orange peel and plenty of garlic cloves. The sauce was thickened with breadcrumbs, a very old-fashioned way of making sauce but delicious nevertheless.

CORDERO AL CHILINDRON
Lamb in Pepper Sauce

We enjoyed this lamb dish in a hotel in Spain but it is also traditional in the South of France, particularly in the Basque country. This is a highly seasoned and very tasty dish.

For 6 people
1½ k/3 lbs lean lamb, cut into 2 oz pieces
3 tbsp olive oil
¾ of a large tin of tomatoes in their juice
2—3 medium-sized, onions
6 garlic cloves
500 g/1 lb green or red peppers (chopped)
1—2 fresh hot chillis (to taste)
½ bottle white wine

Fry the lamb in oil. Do it in two instalments if necessary. Keep aside. In a casserole dish, fry the onion and the whole garlic cloves. To this add the chopped peppers. Finish cooking with all the other ingredients, tomatoes, wine, lamb and the chillis (remove the seeds). Cook slowly for an hour or so. Check the seasoning. This dish can be enjoyed not only in winter but also in summer in spite of its high seasoning and is particularly good served with rice.

COUSCOUS D'AGNEAU
Lamb Couscous

This is no more a French dish than curried lamb is English. It is a tasty legacy from France's links with North Africa, the Maghreb. Like curry it is very much the speciality of a hot

country—spicy, tasty and lively. There are several types, but
the one I like best is *Couscous à l'Agneau*, Lamb Couscous.
Needless to say I do not use spring lamb, but older, more mature
meat from 6 months to 1 year old. This is a dish for plenty
of people, no less than six, and is ideal for an informal party.

For 6 to 8 people
1½—2 kg/3—4 lb best end of neck, sliced
1 kg/2 lb boned shoulder of lamb
1—1½ litres/2—3 pints water
500 g/1 lb couscous—medium gauge
200 g/7 oz chick peas
2 bay leaves
700 g/1½ lb carrots
1 bouquet garni
1 tbsp hot paprika
1 tsp each of ground coriander, cumin, ginger, cinnamon
½ tsp cayenne pepper
5 large onions, sliced and chopped
6—8 garlic cloves
3 large tomatoes
1 medium-sized fennel bulb, sliced
700 g/1½ lb courgettes, thickly sliced
2—3 white turnips cut into quarters
3 large peppers, de-seeded and sliced
3 tbsp olive oil.
A handful of sultanas (optional)
Salt and pepper

Soak the chick peas for a few hours, drain, then simmer for
two hours in water with the bay leaves and salt. This can be
done in advance.

Fry the lamb in oil. Add the onions and when they are just
coloured, cover with water. Add the salt and all the spices and
bring to the boil. After 20 minutes add the vegetables. Keep
cooking for another 30 minutes, then taste the broth. It must
be richly flavoured and spicy. Adjust the seasonings. Having
no *couscoussier* (a special steamer to cook the *couscous*), I place
a colander over the pan with the meat and the vegetables and
put the *couscous* in the colander to steam. Make sure the gap
all around the colander does not let too much steam escape. If

it does, pad it with a tea towel. The *couscous* takes about half an hour to cook, after which it is smoothed carefully by hand with a little oil. With *couscous* becoming popular, the semolina is prepared in such a way nowadays that the cooking is easy and quick. All the relevant instructions are on the package.

The dish is served with the *couscous* grains mixed with sultanas (optional). The meats are piled on one dish. The vegetables are on another with the broth and the chick peas.

To give more fire to *couscous*, a hot dish with harissa is handed round. Harissa, like curry, is a mixture of spices, the main ones being cayenne pepper and red hot peppers. The ground powders are mixed with a little oil. Harissa powder is sold everywhere in France nowadays and in quite a few places in Britain

A sure sign that *couscous* has become part of the French repertoire nowadays is that *charcutiers-traiteurs* (specialised butcher shops selling cooked meals to take away) advertise and sell *couscous*, especially at the weekend. Not long ago, listening to one of my favourite Sunday programmes on the French radio, I heard an interesting piece of information. The Lycée Français in London had received a special accolade. It had been selected by a British good food organisation as the school where they had tasted the best meal. The menu—*couscous*. Could not be more French, commented somebody!

With fine *couscous* make a tasty and easy starter in the style of Lebanese Tabbouleh. Soak the *couscous* in plenty of lemon juice and oil (olive oil if you like), season with salt and hot paprika and mix in a green chilli and some crab meat (tinned or fresh). Sprinkle with flat parsley or coriander to taste. It is not only unusual but good and full of vitamins.

SOME IDEAS FOR ROAST PORK

With very little extra work you can easily give new life to an old recipe. Certain preparations come to mind with roast pork.

Roll the pork, including the ends, in coarse sea salt and keep it for 2 to 3 hours. Wipe off the salt carefully and roast as usual. The pork acquires extra flavour with this short salting. Cooked properly, pork is tender, moist and tasty. Quite often, unfortunately, it is overcooked and becomes dry and unpalatable. The excess of zeal may be due to the fear of under-cooking, and all its dangers.

PORK ROLLED
IN PEPPER

Alternatively roll the roast all over, including the ends, in coarsely ground pepper, *poivre mignonnette*, as used for steak *au poivre*. Press the pepper into the meat with your hands, brown all over and cook as usual. It is simply delicious and not at all overpowering; tasty and appetising whether served hot or cold. A cold roast pork, an orange mayonnaise and a potato salad make a perfect trio at lunch time. It tastes summery even when warmer days are more a promise than a reality.

ORANGE SALAD

ORANGE
MARINADE

OLIVE
MARINADE

I have a special liking for blood oranges; I heard long ago (maybe a myth) that the red markings, rather pronounced at times, are due to a drop of temperature in the growing season—a shiver in the orange grove. To make a spicy orange salad, juicy oranges are best. Peel an orange as if it were an apple, using a sharp knife, so that the flesh is showing to the quick. Slice the oranges and add dressing just before serving (oil and cider vinegar, 3 to 1, salt and pepper). According to the time of year, sprinkle the oranges with chopped chives, shallots or a finely sliced red onion. An orange salad is quick, refreshing and colourful. Scatter a few black olives, whole or chopped. After the long journey north , the olives lose some of their flavour and need reviving—a marinade is the answer, with olive oil, a few crushed coriander seeds or cumin as an alternative), and a little chopped garlic. These olives keep well for quite a long time at room temperature; they make a nice nibble with a drink.

MAYONNAISE À L'ORANGE
Orange Flavoured Mayonnaise

With cold roast pork, home-made mayonnaise is good and well worth making. At home, as a child, it was my duty and privilege to make the mayonnaise; by the age of ten I was a real expert, and if anything went wrong I knew how to save the situation. The oil must be at room temperature, so must the eggs, that is to say, not straight from the fridge. If, through lack of time the planning suffers and the eggs are cold when needed, add a spoonful of hot wine vinegar to the yolks and proceed as usual. When the mayonnaise is ready, mix in the juice of one orange or more if you want it thinner, and the finely grated rind; it adds a fruity taste and a nice tang. (Cold sea trout does well with such a sauce.)

Whenever a French recipe mentions the use of citrus fruit it never fails to say that the fruit must be *non traité* i.e. not sprayed with diphenyl or a similar chemical. It lengthens the life of the fruit in the shops but does no good to one's stomach in the long run. I wipe the fruit with vinegar (malt, because it is cheap) and wash it. I gather that alcohol breaks down the chemicals too, but it would be rather expensive!

SALADE DE POMMES DE TERRE
Potato Salad

For 4 people
½ k/1 lb new potatoes
1 small glass of white wine
6 tbsp oil
2 tbsp vinegar—cider or red wine vinegar
Salt and freshly ground pepper
Spring onions and herbs, chopped

Cook the potatoes—they must remain firm; peel, slice (not too thinly) while warm, add a very small glass of white wine, it helps the moisture and the flavour! Season the vinaigrette with salt and pepper to taste and mix with the potatoes. Before serving, add the onions and herbs (chives, a little sorrel, early dandelion or spring onions, whatever you can find.)

PORC À L'ORANGE
Pork with Orange

This loin of pork cooked in a casserole is tender with a fresh fruity flavour.

For 4 to 6 people
1½ k/3 lb loin of pork
1 tbsp oil
2 oranges (juice and 1 peel cut finely into thin strips)
1 large glass of white wine

½ k/1 lb carrots finely grated.
Salt and pepper
A little butter and sugar

Brown the pork in the oil on all sides, then add the orange juice, white wine, salt, pepper and carrots. The carrots thicken the sauce and blend beautifully with the orange flavour. Blanch the peel of one orange and add to the sauce 30 minutes before the dish is ready. One extra orange or two, peeled, sliced and fried in a little butter with a sprinkling of sugar gives a finishing touch to the dish. Wine can be replaced by more orange juice, sharpened with the juice of 2 lemons.

CARBONADE DE PORC FLAMAND
Flemish Carbonade with Pork

The recipe is better known made with beef. This version, given to me by a Belgian friend, is as good, if not better.

For 4 to 5 people
700 g—1 kg/1½—2 lb lean pork cut into pieces
1½ lb onions
¾ litre/27 fl. oz good ale (the quality is important)
2 bay leaves
1 dsp flour
1 dsp brown sugar
3 tbsp oil and lard
Salt and pepper

Fry the onions gently in a casserole dish until just golden. Add the meat, seal well and sprinkle with flour. Stir for a while and when it begins to colour, slowly pour in the beer, stirring until the sauce thickens. At this point add the bay leaves, seasoning and sugar. Let it cook gently in the oven for 1½ hours with a tight lid on. Check the flavouring before serving.

Optional: 10 minutes or so before the dish is ready, remove the lid and cover the top with slices of French bread, spread on both sides with mustard. Bake in the oven until the top is crunchy. It is a substantial and filling dish; what Colette, the writer, would call *roboratif*. It is perfect in winter and left-overs reheat well.

The friend who gave me the recipe is an imaginative cook who delights in the art of cooking an excellent meal at little cost. It is something I enjoy doing too, a stimulating and rewarding exercise. After such a meal, and as we were rather boasting about this ability, she said, partly serious, partly joking, 'You and I could feed six people with marrow bones!' A daunting exercise, but given a large bone with plenty of marrow . . . food for thought anyway!

ENCHAUD DE PORC
Stuffed Roast Pork

This is a simple recipe which gives wonderful results. It is extremely tasty and good for a buffet, cold dinner, or a picnic.

For 6 people
1½ kg/3 lb boned loin of pork with the belly flap attached
225—350g/8—12 oz sausage meat (fat and lean pork minced coarsely and well seasoned)
100 g/4 oz streaky bacon, finely chopped
1 egg
4 garlic cloves
1 shallot
Parsley and a sprinkling of thyme
Salt and pepper
A glass of white wine
A few bay leaves

Season the pork. Cut each clove of garlic into 3 pieces and, with a sharp knife, make incisions in the meat and push some of the pieces through. For the stuffing mix the sausage meat, the finely chopped bacon, the rest of the garlic and herbs. Bind with the egg and half the glass of wine, making sure that the seasoning is good. Arrange the stuffing inside the flap. Bind this to the pork as tightly as possible and secure with kitchen string. Lay it in a cocotte dish and brown on all sides, then pour the rest of the wine and the same amount of water or stock. Place the bay leaves on top.

Cook in a warm oven (180C/350F/mark 4) without a lid for half an hour, then cover and cook gently for an hour or so, making sure that the pork does not dry up.

When it is ready, remove the strings and arrange in a terrine of appropriate size. Let it cool for 24 hours then slice carefully and serve with a green salad.

BIFTECK TARTARE
Steak Tartare

Steak Tartare is still eaten frequently in France and Switzerland. Traditionally, it is said, horse meat should be used, in which case I will never be a traditionalist!

I made it quite often at home when the children were young having been brought up with the old-fashioned idea that growing children must eat plenty of red meat, raw if possible! They loved it, but I served it in a modified form. As a rule, good quality steak, freshly minced and seasoned, is served on individual plates with the yolk of egg perched on top and the colourful display is completed by a generous spoonful of chopped onion, parsley, gherkins and capers.

I have never served a steak tartare that looked like a Steak Tartare! Mine has always been suitably camouflaged.

For 4 people
450 g/1 lb freshly ground, lean, tender steak
2 egg yolks
250 ml/9 fl.oz vegetable oil
A soupçon of Worcester sauce or Tabasco
1 tsp mustard for the mayonnaise (optional)
1 onion or shallot, finely chopped
5—6 small gherkins
2 spoonfuls drained capers
1 bunch of parsley and chives, finely chopped
Salt and pepper to taste

Make a mayonnaise by slowly adding oil to the egg yolks, stirring constantly. Then add the shallot (or onion), capers, gherkins and parsley and chives. Season to taste.

Mix the mayonnaise with the raw, minced steak and serve on individual plates with very hot, finely cut chips, a green salad, and lemon and tomato quarters arranged around the edge of the dish.

BOEUF À LA PROVENÇALE
Provencal Stew

This is a very tasty dish, needs slow cooking and can be prepared ahead without losing its quality—far from it. Another good point is that it can be served cold and it will have quite a different character and appeal. Orange peel, some olives and herbs give a Provençal accent to beef cooked in wine. Traditionally it is served hot with a larger than usual macaroni, grated cheese and a good measure of tasty sauce.

For 8 to 10 people
1½—2 kg/4—5 lbs silverside or shoulder fillet
5—6 garlic cloves
Bouquet garni (2 bay leaves, plenty of thyme and parsley)
6 carrots
3 onions, or onions and shallots
100 g/4 oz good quality black olives—stoned
Peel of 1 orange. Seville orange is traditional but not imperative
200 g/7—8 oz streaky bacon cut rather thick
1 small glass good red wine vinegar
300 g/10 oz smooth pork rind (optional)
2 or 3 medium sized very ripe tomatoes, peeled
1 bottle of full bodied red wine—Provençal, if possible
3—4 tbsp olive oil

Cut the meat into cubes and marinate with the wine, the wine vinegar, sliced carrots, herbs, onions and shallots. Leave overnight, and preferably for 24 hours.

Cut the bacon into small cubes and fry lightly. Add the meat, patted dry, having strained the marinade into a separate bowl. Fry without browning. The vegetables come next—fry very gently, and when they are soft add the marinade, the orange peel and peeled tomatoes. Pork rind gives it a smoother and richer sauce and good protection for the lengthy cooking. Make sure to singe it carefully if necessary, parboil for a few minutes and line the bottom of the dish before adding the other ingredients. Cook in a large cast iron or earthenware dish—a tight lid is essential. The wine must cover the meat. Add stock or water if necessary. Bring to the boil and cook slowly in the oven at 177C/350F/mark 4 for at least 3 to 4 hours. This slow cooking 111 will make the meat very tender. Add the olives 30 minutes before it is ready.

All this can be done ahead. When dinner approaches, reheat and enjoy this very tasty *Boeuf à la Provençale*. If the liquid is a little scant, add more of the same wine before reheating. It will enliven the sauce and freshen it up.

Serve with small new potatoes in season, fresh macaroni or noodles, croûtons fried in olive oil and a crisp green salad with a few slivers of black olives, marinated beforehand in a little olive oil, fresh thyme and garlic.

BEEF
TERRINE

To turn this winter dish into a cool summer one, add early on in the cooking one calf's foot cut in half, or 2 fresh pig's trotters. (Pork sold at the butcher is usually young and the bones are gelatinous). Failing this, use commercial gelatine, according to the quantity of liquid, the temperature etc. Pork rind will already have helped the texture, if used.

Choose a rectangular dish (as if making a terrine), the meat will slice more easily. Pack the cooled stew into the dish and put in the fridge. With a little time to spare, make the dish more attractive by setting a few cooked sliced carrots and some olives at the bottom of the dish (optional). Turn out and decorate with parsley, tomato slices, chives and olives.

Choux à Gogo

CHOUX À GOGO
Cabbages Galore

This is the last of the winter days, cold and nippy, but clear and bright. The patch of Savoy cabbages is sparkling in the morning sun. The wavy outside leaves spread out like stiff collars with dewdrops hanging all around. I gaze silently, bend my head right, then left, and at the change of angle, a drop lights up here, another there. It is fun to be seven or eight and play with the sun and these morning glories.

When a leaf is broken off the cabbage, the smell is strong and pungent, a winter smell. These outside leaves were fed to the domestic rabbit (known as *lapin de chou*), a favourite winter fodder. Given a chance, wild rabbits, *lapins de garenne*, show even more enthusiasm, choosing the best cabbage in the garden. Would their noses quiver at the cabbages, stripped and conveniently wrapped for the shops! In France, the legend of babies born out of cabbages (their rotundity no doubt inspired it) is dying out; nowadays the facts of life being told at an early age, cabbages and storks have become redundant, for better or for worse. But not quite it seems. A nineteen year old French girl recently told me that 'Little boys were born out of cabbages and little girls out of roses'. Her grandmother had said so when she was a little girl—'sugar and spice and all things nice', Gallic style. From this nursery legend comes, no doubt, the affectionate *'mon chou, mon petit chou'*, used by the French; though it has nothing to do with gastronomic delights. *The Larousse Gastronomique* assumes that the Hebrews did not know about cabbages since they did not mention them in the Bible. It is known that the Romans and the Greeks loved them but had to be content with small ones. Modern varieties like the *Savoy* would have made them very envious, especially the Romans, who kept praising their many virtues. Among other things they believed that cabbages lessened the effects of generous libations; they had to be eaten before and after the feast—a treat! I would prefer a *chou à la crème* (a cream bun).

Cato, a serious thinker, who had among other things, a legal mind, was the champion of the cabbage; the best food ever, 115 he claimed, because of its healing properties. Marie-Antoinette Mulot, a well known French herbalist, is almost as enthusiastic: 'it is a source of vitamins and minerals (calcium, magnesium and sulphur) and has many curative properties'. One of her simple remedial recipes is a raw cabbage salad before a rich meal to help digestion. It is tasty, crunchy, and colourful (red cabbage, or a mixture, side by side), and was a delight to me as a child. In winter, when salads are scarce and expensive, it adds variety and vitamins at a small price.

SALADE AUX CHOUX CRUS
Raw Cabbage Salad

For 4 people
½ k/1 lb cabbage (red and/or white)
Vinaigrette (made with caraway seeds and mustard)

Remove tough or damaged outside leaves and hard stalks. Slice very finely, season with a sharp vinaigrette a couple of hours before the salad is required to soften it. If using red cabbage, the vinegar is essential to keep the colour. Alternatively, the sliced cabbage can be parboiled for one minute, cooled under the tap and drained. Taste and texture change slightly. Some people like it better.

VINAIGRETTE   A vinaigrette dressing is made basically with three tablespoons of oil and one of vinegar; i.e. a proportion of three to one, though there may be slight variations according to taste. The addition of sugar to a vinaigrette dressing has caused my eyebrows to rise many a time. The use of acid malt vinegar was, no doubt, responsible for this habit, which is at last disappearing. Apple or wine vinegar are far better to sharpen the flavour without killing it.

Recently, on a very simple menu in France, I chose cabbage salad. The diet of the previous days dictated my choice! I was pleasantly surprised with it. In individual bowls garnished with lettuce leaves was finely sliced white cabbage, mixed with thin strips of raw carrots, peeled grapefruit segments, walnuts and a lemon dressing. Easy and refreshing.

Nowadays we can find cabbages of all types, all sizes, and
practically for all seasons, with a peak in winter. They are

moderately priced, versatile and plentiful. Traditional recipes
are endless; more sophisticated ones have appeared for our
pleasure and sometimes to our surprise. Cabbage has gone up
in the cooking world! Lengthy cooking is no longer the rule;
shorter cooking keeps in the vitamins, attracts more supporters
and originates new ideas. Communal staircases, schools or can-
teens should never again spread the unsavoury tales of ruined
cabbages and ruined appetites.

My favourite variety for its looks and its flavour is the Savoy,
chou de Milan. It tastes better after the early frost and makes
splendid stuffed cabbage and winter soups.

A thick cabbage soup is not a child's idea of a feast. Adults
are more partial to it. Not long ago, in rural areas in winter,
cabbage soup provided the most usual meal: soup with vegetables and meat, in varying quantities; at worst a piece of
streaky bacon; at best, for special occasions, a substantial variety
of meats.

POTÉE
A complete meal in itself

For 6 people or more
½ kg/1 lb carrots
1 kg/2 lb cabbage cut into quarters
3 leeks
2 onions with cloves stuck in each of them
250 g/½ lb swede
3—4 white turnips (small)
2 sticks celery
1 small celeriac
1 kg/2 lb potatoes (optional)
4 cloves garlic
250 g/½ lb garlic sausage
250 g/½ lb lean salt pork
250 g/½ lb streaky bacon in one thick slice, smoked if preferred
500 g/1 lb boiling ham
1 knuckle of pork or hand of pork

Keep the knuckle of pork in salt for a couple of days to improve
the flavour (wipe and rinse well before cooking). The salting 117

process is mentioned in the chapter on sausages. For bigger
crowds and richer flavour add a boiling fowl and more
vegetables.

Fill a large pan with 3 litres/5 pints of water. Add the meats
(except the sausage), bring to the boil for about an hour, skim-
ming whenever necessary. Add the vegetables, but keep the cabbage and the potatoes for later—another 30 minutes and they
will go into the *potée* with the sausage. Half an hour later the
meal is ready (around two hours gentle cooking in total). Check
the seasoning: little salt is required since the meats provide
plenty. Remove fat with kitchen paper if necessary.

Strained off, the stock makes a tasty soup with thin slices of
stale or slightly toasted, country-style bread, white or brown,
added to each bowl. Serve with grated cheese. In my part of
France it is Cantal cheese, similar to mature farmhouse cheddar,
and very ancient in the cheese lineage too. Pepper from the mill
is a must in such a robust soup.

The meats and the vegetables make the main course with
mustards and pickles (onions, gherkins etc). As a pleasant
accompaniment prepare a vinaigrette sauce with a chopped
boiled egg (1 or 2 according to numbers), finely chopped shallot
or onion, 1 tablespoon chopped capers or pickled gherkins.

This is a whole meal, simple hearty fare that tells of hard-
working people, hard winters and rustic surroundings. It is a
revitalising antidote after too much elaborate cooking, too many
subtle sauces. There is a need for such dishes—some restaurants
do very well by specialising in them—it cleans a jaded palate
and reminds us of earlier, unsophisticated ways. Continuity is
reasserted, a reassuring thought amidst all the change.

ROUZOLE
Fried Stuffing

To add more interest to a simple cabbage soup, without overtax-
ing the budget, a farci can be served with it. Word for word,
it is a stuffing. In the south it is sometimes called a *rouzoule*,
or *roussole* because it must be nicely fried beforehand.

For 6 people

2 eggs

150 g/5 oz stale bread (moistened with a little water and
    squeezed dry)
1 tbsp chopped parsley
2—3 finely chopped garlic cloves
1 finely chopped onion
300 g/10 oz home-made sausage meat
2 tbsp oil
Pepper and a little salt
Optional extras: chives or sorrel

Mix all the ingredients thoroughly, except the oil, and check the seasonings. Heat the oil in the frying pan and pour the mixture onto it, spreading and flattening it with the back of a spoon. Cook on one side until nicely coloured. Slide onto a large flat dish then cook on the other side. After a few minutes, reduce the heat and finish cooking (with the lid on) for 20 to 25 minutes in all. To serve, slide the *farci* onto a flat dish of appropriate size, serve after the soup with the vegetables from the original stock and with a salad. To be more traditional, cut into smaller pieces, share between the bowls and pour the soup over it.

SOUPE DE CHOU GRATINÉE
French Cabbage Soup

For 6 people
1—1½ kg/2—3 lb green or white cabbage (sliced)
1 bay leaf
2 onions with 1 clove
2 carrots
Plenty of bones (beef, ham etc)—or meat stock cubes on busy
    days with a glass of white wine. My purist and intransigent
    friends would frown on this.
500 g/1 lb grated white farmhouse cheddar (or half cheddar and
    half mature Gouda or Gruyère)
225 g/½ lb crusty French bread, stale or toasted.
Salt and pepper
3—4 pints water

Put the bones and onions, carrots and bay leaf into the water and boil for one hour. Add the sliced cabbage and cook for a further 30 minutes or so. Then remove the bones, the onion,

carrots and bay leaf. Fill a gratinée dish (earthenware preferably) with layers of cabbage, sliced bread, cheese and freshly
ground pepper. Salt moderately (the cheese provides plenty).
Fill with the stock, up to the top. Cook in a hot oven (220C/425F/
mark 7) for 20 minutes. Sprinkle with 2 tablespoons grated
cheese (kept aside) and cook until the top is golden and crisp.

This cabbage soup is simple, tasty and different from the
traditional onion gratinée, and extremely popular. One of my
extrovert French friends, a southerner and a rugby enthusiast,
gave me this recipe. The *best*, he said, if you use plenty of freshly
ground pepper and cheese. In a word, be generous.

When men turn into Sunday cooks they do not believe in
short measure or parsimony. Once in a small French restaurant,
a few men at the next table were discussing food and cooking.
The exchange was lively, listening was irresistable. 'Moi', said
one emphatically, 'when I bake a fruit tart it is as big as a cart
wheel'. His arm drew in the air the imaginary tart and it was
no ordinary tart! In the farms of the past with built-in bread
ovens or kindly village bakers, tarts were baked on a large scale
for special occasions like marriages, harvesting or even funerals.
One look at them, and the heart rejoiced. A Belgian friend
remembers visiting country cousins and these huge confections
delighted her; ripples of brown sugar (*cassonade*) and butter
bubbling in crusty pastry—*whirlpools of happiness* her father
called them. The exclamations of admiration never persuaded
the farmer's wife to part with the recipe—her secret. She took
it with her to her grave. Many attempts by my friend never
succeeded in recreating the special tart—the subtle flavours of
the past had gone, or is it that the magic moments of youth
never return?

CHOU FARCI
Stuffed Cabbage

This is a traditional winter dish, the reward at the end of a cold
gloomy day. Even sun-worshippers would agree that such
touches make winter quite bearable. In days gone by, a stuffed
cabbage cooked slowly with the soup in the pot. It cooks more
easily and evenly in the oven in a casserole dish of appropriate

size; the flavour is even better as none of it is lost in the broth. The stuffing varies from region to region, from one cook to another. The best known is possibly the *sou-fassum* from Provence. the one I prefer is a recipe from my area!

For 6 to 8 people
1 Savoy cabbage—(about 1 kg/2 lb)
A few slices of streaky bacon (or pork rind)
Stuffing
300 g/10 oz home-made sausage meat
   Instead of ground pork in the sausage use beef, veal and
      chicken or pork mixed with chestnuts
3 cloves garlic, chopped
1 small bunch parsley (the flat variety for a better flavour)
3 eggs
100 g/4 oz stale breadcrumbs
Salt and plenty of freshly ground pepper

For vegetarian stuffing choose a selection from: partially cooked rice, spinach, chopped mushrooms, eggs, nuts, chestnuts, onions and , of course, breadcrumbs. Mix all the ingredients together and keep to one side.

COOKING LIQUID

2 glasses stock mixed with either light beer or dry white wine
1 small carrot
1 onion
2 slices bacon (chopped)
2 or 3 tomatoes or 1 small tin

Remove damaged and tough outside leaves from the cabbage. Blanch it whole for 10 to 15 minutes. Cool and drain. Open up the leaves gently, remove the heart, chop it finely and add to the stuffing. Replace the heart with the stuffing and distribute the rest in between each leaf. Tie with kitchen string to hold the cabbage together and, if possible, wrap in a cloth; the cabbage will keep its shape and contents better and it will be easier to take out of the cooking dish.

   A cast iron casserole dish of appropriate size is ideal for slow and even cooking. Soften the chopped onion and carrot in a little oil with the chopped bacon. Add the hot stock (or whatever liquid is chosen). Two or three ripe tomatoes (or a small tin) add extra flavour and colour. Line the dish with the streaky bacon or pork rind, fatty side down, then pour in the sauce. Lay the cabbage on top and cook in a fairly hot oven (190C/375F/mark 5) for about 2 hours, lid on.

Arrange on a heated serving dish (removing the string and muslin). Cut into portions and serve very hot, with some of the sauce from the bottom of the dish (sieved preferably). Hand around mustard—I do like the flavour of red pepper mustard, if available.

A quicker version can be made by preparing the casserole dish as before but simply filling with layers of sliced cabbage and stuffing. Before putting the lid on, remember to add 3 to 4 ripe tomatoes and one glass of stock or white wine or beer. The dish cooks more quickly (an hour or so) simmered over a low heat on top of the cooker, or in the oven for more even cooking.

Alternatively, individual leaves blanched beforehand can be filled, rolled and arranged side by side in an oven dish on a layer of onion and carrot as previously described. Alternate dark leaves and pale leaves. The cooking is much shorter and the fillings can be based on partially cooked rice for vegetarian mixture adding spinach, beet leaves (*bette ou poirée*), cheese and chopped eggs, for example.

When cabbage is plentiful and variety in the menu is an incentive for the one who cooks and the one who eats, *gratin de chou* (cabbage gratine) rings the change. It can be a vegetarian dish or a more substantial one with chopped bacon (parboiled) or chopped ham (100 g/4 oz)

GRATIN DE CHOU
Cabbage with Cheese

For 6 people
1 cabbage — 1½ k/3 lb
225 g/8 oz grated cheese (mature Gouda, farmhouse Cheddar or good Emmental)
½ litre/17 fl.oz creamy milk
2 eggs
Pepper
Nutmeg to flavour

The cheese being salty, use little or no salt. Slice the cabbage finely and parboil for 2 or 3 minutes then drain. In a well buttered gratin dish, spread a layer of the cabbage and a layer of grated cheese, ending with cabbage. Mix the yolks with the warm milk, heat but do not boil and pour over the vegetables. Bake for 30 minutes or so in a warm oven.

Alternatively, make a cheese sauce with the yolks, cheese and milk, mix with the cabbage and cover with home-made breadcrumbs dotted lightly with butter. Bake as before and crispen under the grill for a minute or two.

In another chapter, *Saucisse de Toulouse*, I mentioned lightly cooked cabbage to serve with meat or fish. Small tender cabbage, quartered, parboiled and drained, is delicious heated in a little butter or cream, or mixed with meat juices around a roast for example. Basil goes well with lightly cooked, tender summer cabbage. A few ripe skinned tomatoes (or a small tin) give extra colour and flavour.

Because lightly cooked cabbage does not have a pronounced flavour, contemporary chefs and cooks use it with assurance or even panache, with unexpected or sophisticated preparations. Without going overboard and mixing everything together, it is good to see that cooking adapts and changes. It is very much alive!

Panaché
de Legumes

PANACHÉ DE LÈGUMES
Some Ideas for Vegetables

I was brought up by a mother with exceptionally green fingers, in an area where the temperature was warm from May onwards. Fruit and vegetables were plentiful, varied and always picked at their peak. I loved their continuous succession from small tender radishes in early spring to perfectly flavoured and scented Charentais melons in summer. Later, ripe figs, sagging and ready to drop, overflowed with honeyed juice. My mother would select one at a glance and pick it for me. 'Try this one. It is pure honey—*C'est du miel*', she would say.

On a hilly farm in France an elderly farmer presented me with a beautiful pumpkin, and turned poet to tell me the merits of this aristocrat of the species—and indeed, it revealed a deep **PUMPKINS** orange colour inside, a most delicate texture and flavour, plus versatility. We had variations on a theme! One slice, stewed first in very little water with sugar and lemon and with an appealing and colourful creamy custard made from vanilla, egg, rich milk and nutmeg. Thin lemon shortbread made a nice contrast to the creaminess of the pudding, as would crisp *sablés* (a French version, one could say). Another slice was stewed and blended into a caramel egg custard, with a little flour for thickening and fresh ginger. (Ginger is for me a relatively recent discovery—as **GINGER** it would be for most French people. I confess to an instant addiction to the fruity and spicy flavour). Any leftover pumpkin can be cut into pieces and roasted with the Christmas turkey, an idea from a New Zealand friend—it was delicious with a good sprinkling of pepper. That year the festive bird (always a hen turkey, free-range) appeared flanked by a colourful trio; sautéed brussel sprouts, roast pumpkin, and spicy red cabbage, cooked for so long that it tasted almost like a chutney, *confit de chou rouge*! **TURKEY**

In France, in the shops or the markets in springtime there are bunches of new onions for sale. They are bound together by their bright green stems. A casserole of tender young onions **SPRING ONION** mixed with new spring carrots is one of my favourite dishes **CASSEROLE** at that time of year. A knob of butter, a little thyme from the garden a few green olives and gentle cooking, is all you need. 127

In the autumn the last of the tomatoes were gathered, still green, before the frosts. The larger ones can be fried like ripe tomatoes. The flavour is excellent and so is the texture. The smaller ones, sliced, mixed with sugar and finely sliced lemon, make, in my opinion, a superlative autumn jam. The pale green, translucent confiture is appealing and has a fresh taste.

CONFITURE DE TOMATES VERTES
Green Tomato Jam

1 kg/2 lb tomatoes, chopped
2—3 lemons, finely sliced
800 g/1¾ lb sugar

Mix together in a large bowl and leave overnight. Cook the next day until set; pour in jars and seal well. This recipe is popular in France, as it must have been in Britain years ago, since it is mentioned so often in old cookery books.

CHOUX DE BRUXELLES
Brussel Sprouts

Brussel sprouts are a versatile and useful vegetable. Lightly cooked in a little salty water, then sautéed in fat (oil and butter or good lard), they are especially good. The flavour of the outside leaves, which turn a little crisp and golden, is delicious. A spoonful of roasted sesame seeds added to the sautéed sprouts gives a nutty flavour, unusual and good; or quite simply, a good sprinkling of freshly ground black pepper. With a little nutmeg, cream and a yolk, they take on a new look and a new flavour. They could also be sprinkled with Gruyère cheese and gratinéed. For a light attractive soup add some light stock with a little cream to the puréed sprouts. Serve with tiny croûtons or sprinkle with very crisp crunchy bacon. Do not forget the pepper mill.

Globe artichokes are one of my favourite vegetables. In spite of several attempts to grow them in Scotland, hard frosts have defeated me. The artichokes that were ready to eat at the end of May in France would be ready for picking here at the very end of summer. However wonderful they were, the waiting had been too long and too frustrating. I was not born patient . . .

Young tender artichokes enjoyed with Spanish friends living near Valencia made me feel almost lyrical and beautifully contented at the time. Tiny, tender asparagus served on the next day with a token of creamy scrambled eggs were almost as exciting.

ARTICHAUTS À LA BARIGOULE
Artichoke Hearts in Wine

This is made with tender artichokes cooked gently with cubes of smoked streaky bacon, garlic, parsley, thyme and a large glass of white wine. If the artichokes are older and bigger, as they usually are when bought in Britain, only use the heart, cut into quarters. Rub them with lemon juice as they tend to darken quickly.

For 4 people
1 large artichoke heart per person
200 ml/1 glass white wine
8 cloves garlic
225 g/½ lb smoked streaky bacon, thickly cut
2 tbsp olive oil
Thyme
Salt and pepper

In a casserole dish, sauté the bacon with the olive oil, add the garlic, then the artichokes. Pour in the wine and enough water to come half way up the artichokes. Add thyme and seasoning and cook slowly for about 40 minutes, or until tender. Serve on its own. Crusty bread will help to enjoy the last of the tasty sauce. The last time I enjoyed *artichauts barigoule* was with my niece in Corsica. She had been taught by her grandmother, my own mother. It is very pleasing to see cooking perpetuated in the kitchen from generation to generation.

BETTE OU POIRÉE
Swiss chard

This belongs to the beet family. The green leaves are tasty, refreshing and allowed in a diet when spinach is forbidden. This is a very ancient vegetable, not only in France but in Britain too. While it is very popular in France, especially in the south, it seems to have gone out of fashion altogether here. It is a pity since it grows very well, even in Scotland. When all is quiet and dormant in the garden it starts growing leaves again before going to seed. The white rib is tender and delicious and used quite differently from the leaves; two vegetables in one. In the south of France they are sold in bundles, or as a whole plant and quite cumbersome to carry in a shopping bag! When the white stems are very large and fleshy, they must be peeled, in the same way as rhubarb. Slice, blanch for a minute or two and cook with a little butter, or add the juices from a roast and simmer for a few minutes. They can be served with a tomato sauce, gratiné, mixed with a cheesy white sauce, or simply layered with cheese and single cream.

To make sure the white ribs do not darken, add 1 tablespoon of flour to the water used for blanching, or lemon juice.

POIREAUX VINAIGRETTE
Leeks Vinaigrette

For 4 to 5 people
1 kg/2 lb leeks
Vinaigrette
2 hard boiled eggs

Clean the leeks and tie into bundles with string. Trim off most of the green part to use for soup. Cook the white parts in salted boiling water for about 10 to 15 minutes according to size, until just tender. Drain, cool and remove the strings. Arrange in a long, flat dish. Pour vinaigrette over the leeks, flavoured with a little mustard. Decorate with finely chopped boiled eggs.

AUBERGINES AU JAMBON
Aubergine Sandwiched with Ham

Peel and slice the aubergine (1 cm/½ in). Sprinkle with salt. After a couple of hours they lose a lot of moisture and bitterness. Dry with kitchen paper and sandwich with lean ham, cut to size. Flatten these sandwiches slightly with a rolling pin. Dip them in a beaten egg, roll in flour and cook in oil like fritters. Drain on kitchen paper to get rid of the excess fat. Serve very hot on their own with a sprinkling of chopped or fried parsley. I make a variation with cheese (using Gruyère, or mature Gouda). Serve with a good tomato sauce flavoured with basil. A tomato and red pepper sauce is another tasty summer accompaniment.

POIVRONS
Peppers

Peppers, red, green, or mixed, are wonderful as a summer starter. Grilled, peeled, cut into strips and served cold, they are excellent with tasty vinaigrette sauce—salt and pepper, a touch of garlic, a sprinkling of basil or mint. Using lemon juice instead of vinegar is even better. It is an attractive and colourful start to a meal, easy to prepare and has a sophisticated, sunny flavour.

To cook the peppers, lay them under a hot grill, and when the skins turn frankly black and well-charred, turn onto the other side to obtain the same result. Wrap in paper (brown bags are best, thick and strong)—the steam inside quickly helps to loosen the whole of the skin.

Grilled sardines served with green peppers is a very tasty combination. It used to be cheap in Portugal. In a 'nice' hotel at the seaside we had to plead with them to cook it for us. Eventually they agreed, but with reservations. 'Food only fit for the poor,' they said. Nonsense, we thought, enjoying the combination.

HARICOTS SECS
Dried Beans

Purées made with lentils or beans are a change from potato purée; the flavours are excellent, the protein content high. Soak the lentils in cold water for a few hours then drain. Put them in some stock flavoured with a couple of carrots, an onion with cloves in it, parsley stems and 1 or 2 cloves of garlic. When the lentils are soft and still hot, pour off the excess liquid and purée with a *mouli-légumes* or a mixer. Add butter, cream or olive oil according to taste and some herbs or whatever flavour you want to achieve and in keeping with the dish it is served with. Season to taste.

Similar purées can be prepared with flageolets; Lima beans are especially good (pale green with a fine skin) and make a smooth, delicate purée. Soak for the night. Start the cooking in cold water. Add the same vegetables as used to flavour the lentils and make sure that the beans are fully covered with liquid. The cooking time depends on the age of the beans. The best I remember were the ones that grew in the garden, and were picked in the pod before drying up. No soaking is required in this case. When the beans are ready, purée and flavour with olive oil; season with pepper. The addition of cream is very traditional. A mild garlicky flavour can be achieved by adding more cloves half way through the cooking of the beans.

A couple of grilled or parboiled green peppers (skin removed) puréed with flageolet beans make a lovely, combination. Sprinkle with finely chopped parsley or a little basil. The traditional vegetable to accompany a leg of lamb is beans. A purée flavoured with garlic or peppers would make a change.

In my part of France beans were used a lot with pork sausage and winter soups. For funerals, there would always be a dish of beans baking slowly in the oven, in readiness for the mourners.

CONSERVES AU VINAIGRE
Pickles

As a child I could not resist home-made pickled gherkins. I liked their sharp flavour and the crunchy bite. They were kept in large glass jars. Once I was caught by my mother indulging in my secret passion. She threatened me of a dire fate and I listened with some concern to the story of the overweight girl who decided to slim and drink vinegar—she died of consumption. The story must have been greatly exaggerated but the result was the same—I did not pinch so many gherkins. My oldest nieces had a worse passion. In the autumn, large white grapes were pickled in sweetened brandy or *eau de vie*—a nice, powerful combination. Eventually one of these jars was found half empty and she confessed to the thefts—two or three at a time when she passed the cupboard where they were kept. Her grandfather (my father) listening to her confession was rather understanding. He had done it all much earlier and when he was younger.

His parents owned a farm and one summer afternoon while they were working not far away, he was told to have a rest in the house and look after his younger brother. My father must have been seven and his brother only three or four. All went well for a while and then mischief started quite innocently. He was thirsty and hungry and plain water did not appeal. He went to fetch the bottle of red wine, and poured a glass for each of them which he sweetened with plenty of sugar and they dipped bread in it. The plain wine, harsh for a young child's taste buds, had become a syrup, most enjoyed on a hot afternoon. When mother returned she found her junior sound asleep under a fir tree by the house. My father was leaning against the trunk saying repeatedly, 'The tree keeps going round'. Alarmed, she discovered the truth when she entered the kitchen.

CORNICHONS AU VINAIGRE
Pickled Gherkins

This is one of the best known condiments in France, the equivalent, maybe, of pickled onions here, or chutney. They are served with cold meats of any kind, and of course, with terrines (liver, game etc). Gherkins belong to the cucumber family — mini version. Like cucumber they thrive on warmth and water, and in those conditions can be grown in the greenhouse or a sheltered garden. The bought variety is quite expensive, salty and pickled in strong vinegar. Home-made pickled gherkins are, to my taste, much better. They can be pickled in hot or cold vinegar. In cold vinegar, they keep their bright colour. Pickled in wine vinegar, the flavour is perfect, but unless using strong wine vinegar the acidity is not high enough to allow lengthy keeping. To ordinary wine vinegar add a little malt vinegar or reduce by boiling.

Pick small gherkins, 2 to 3 inches in length, rub with a cloth or kitchen paper. Sprinkle with sea salt and leave for the night. In the morning wipe the salt off each gherkin and fill a glass or earthenware jar. Add 2 or 3 pickling onions, a few peppercorns and cover with the vinegar of your choice and keep in a cool place for 6 weeks at least.

When using hot vinegar (boiling point) pour over the gherkins, and leave for 48 hours. Repeat the process (bringing the vinegar to the boil) and pour over the gherkins again. Top up with extra vinegar if necessary and wait for six weeks at least before using. In the *Poule au Pot* chapter, I gave a simple recipe for pickled cherries. Here is one for pickled plums.

PRUNES AU VINAIGRE
Pickled Plums

1 kg/2 lb plums, barely ripe
250 g/½ lb sugar
2 cloves
½ litre wine vinegar
5 cm/2 in cinnamon stick

Make a syrup of the sugar, cloves, vinegar and cinnamon. It must boil first for a couple of minutes. Prick the plums all over with a fine needle, leave a little of the stem. Fill a jar with them and slowly pour the spicy vinegar syrup over the plums. Close the jar and start all over again with the same syrup two days later. Make sure the plums are well covered with vinegar—add more if necessary. Wait patiently for six weeks or so before you eat them.

CHAMPIGNONS SAUVAGES
Wild Mushrooms

Once experienced, the pleasure of picking mushrooms becomes compulsive. Buying them at local markets does not give such a thrill. Wild mushrooms could be found once in English markets too. The innate pleasure of hunting for food, gathering nature's offerings whenever possible, is still a strong instinct in modern man. If not over-picked or disturbed, mushrooms come back in the same spot year after year. One or two old wizards in the village knew all the right places—a well kept secret—and the right time. When they returned with a basketful the word went round in a flash and everybody took to the woods, *à pied, à bicyclette ou en voiture.* Soon the powerful and irresist-

able smell of frying cèpes escaped from open windows into the

street—a temptation that must have led shoppers to buy a few,
whatever the price.

Come summer or autumn when heavy rains followed a hot spell, my father often took me with him to pick mushrooms in the local forest—a *départementale* (the property and responsibility of the Region). Whenever I went with my father the first thing he did on entering the forest was to find a strong, suitably sized stick for me. It was a multi-purpose stick: for probing carefully and gently through the tangle of leaves and twigs without damaging the mycelium below the surface, for avoiding and fending off any possible encounters such as adders and eventually to serve as a prop—the perfect tool.

Discovering the first mushroom was, and still is, like a small miracle. *Blasé* is a word unknown to the 'aficionado'. The bountiful years, when everybody found and ate plenty, were remembered like vintage years. In our area it was mainly cèpes and some *oronges* (Caesar's mushrooms).

My mother was the specialist for those beautiful and delicate mushrooms. What was not eaten was bottled or dried. Nowadays some would be kept in the deep-freeze for frying. These are best cooked in hot fat—like deep-frozen chips. With a supply for most of the year, it felt like having a treasure. In winter the pleasure of eating wild mushrooms brightened up the dullest day. It was time to reminisce about the picking, maybe boast a little—the hunter's privilege

Having said so much about the delights of picking and eating mushrooms, I must give some advice. The ones bought in French markets are quite safe; they are checked beforehand by an *expert* (a specialist) on mushrooms. Any chemist in France is happy to look through your basket of mushrooms and tell you if they are all safe. Otherwise pick only what you know well and cannot mistake for a dangerous or deadly species. A good mushroom guide is a great help and there are quite a few books on the subject. A portion of our chanterelle harvest goes to friends, the *cognoscenti*: the trusting and the adventurous, the latter being reassured to know that the giant variety, a poisonous type, favours warmer climates and the shade of the olive trees.

Going back to my early childhood, I remember some details of a mushroom poisoning although the name of the victim eludes me. She lived on a farm a couple of miles from the village and she survived her ordeal, not only from the poisoning but also from the treatment. The doctor, called in the night, gave the very ill woman his instant medicine. He ordered that a rabbit be killed and gutted. The emptied but unwashed innards were cleaned and chopped. She had to eat the plateful, luckily being too unwell to care. The neighbour attending her could not help but enquire about the taste of the medicine: 'It is rather slimy', was the reply. Rabbits are immune to the type of poisonous mushrooms she had eaten! The linings of their guts secrete a substance that breaks down the poisons. Once cooked it is worthless. The thought of the cure may have led people to prudence. Whether the doctor acted of his own accord in an emergency, or whether there were precendents in medical history, my story cannot tell. The old doctor died not all that long ago, practising into his eighties.

Earlier I mentioned *oronges* or Caesar's mushrooms, *Amanités des Césars*. I must now tell the story of the most famous or infamous poisoning by mushrooms. The Caesar who loved these delicacies was Claudius Tiberius. His gourmet tastes were to lead to his downfall. Agrippina, his second wife (after the notorious Messalina) prepared a dish of his favourite mushrooms: he ate them, enjoyed them, and died. Nero, Agrippina's son, succeeded to the throne and that is why she had poisoned Claudius, by adding the juice of the deadly deathcap. Unlike most mushrooms the signs of poisoning are not obvious for a while and when the symptoms appear it is too late. Kidneys and liver are beyond recovery. The agony is terrible, whilst lucidity remains unimpaired to the end. Crime does not pay: Agrippina was murdered in her son's order, and so it went on.

When you know one or two mushrooms well—no need to be too ambitious at the beginning—pick them with care, always. They are alive and delicate. Do not damage the mycelium which is quite close to the surface. Do not destroy the ones that you do not like or do not know. When I find an edible but overgrown mushroom which is past its prime, I scatter pieces all round, hoping to start new breeding grounds, just like the sower with his seeds (or spores in the case of mushrooms). Always leave some mushrooms behind to ensure continuity for future years. As a rule mushroom pickers are quite secretive and possessive
about the places they know, but they will be delighted to share

some of their finds with others.

When I was talking about mushrooms in Scotland with an
hotelier he told me a delightful story. For one season he had
an Italian waiter on his staff who 'knew his mushrooms'. In
his time off he went looking for them—the small woods with
mature oaks and beeches looked promising. He found plenty
and made many people happy that year. Before he returned to
Italy, he was asked by the proprietor where the mushrooms
could be found. 'Sorry, signor, I cannot tell you: it is my secret',
replied Mario, and went back home without telling a soul—rich
with a useless treasure.

For simple cooking, chanterelles are fried and served on toast
with salt and a generous sprinkling of freshly ground pepper.
Chopped bacon added to them is excellent . This is the way
we most enjoy the first picking of the season, carrying the strong,
unmistakable flavour of the woods. Sometimes chopped garlic
and parsley are added to the fried chanterelles. This is a traditional and tasty addition called a *persillade* and fills the kitchen PERSILLADE
with appetising smells. Chopped shallots or onion can replace
the garlic for a less pungent flavour, or simply for a change.
More elaborate cooking comes later with cream, game and terrines. One of our Scottish friends prepared a delicious chanterelle and tomato soup. The texture was velvety (no flour
needed), the taste delicious. On a high class menu in France
it would have read *velouté de chanterelles à la tomate*, and the
magic word would have justified the high price.

RECETTE DE BASE POUR GIROLLES
Basic recipe for Chanterelles

Clean, cut off the stalk end and wash quickly to avoid soaking.
Cook over a low heat in a pan with no water and with the lid
on until the excess water comes out. At this stage drain it off—it
is quicker—or keep cooking until the water has evaporated.
Then fry like most other mushrooms but for longer. Chanterelles do well with a good seasoning of salt and plenty of pepper (garlic, parsley and bacon blend very well, and boost the
flavour). After frying, a spoonful of thick cream warmed
through adds some sophistication. These make a tasty
accompaniment for meat and game.

GIROLLES À L'HUILE ET AU VINAIGRE
Pickled Chanterelles

Chanterelles can be deep-frozen for the winter supply or pickled in oil and vinegar; the recipe comes from Aveyron, a part of France where chanterelles are plentiful. This combination gives a mild and versatile result. Small cèpes can be prepared in the same way. Clean 750 g/1½ lbs chanterelle, sprinkle generously with salt, to get rid of all the water, leave for 5 to 6 hours. Pat dry with absorbent paper. They will look limp and thinner. Mix 3 glasses of oil to one of vinegar (a two to one proportion will give a sharper flavour). Bring to the boil, add the mushrooms and keep boiling gently for 15 to 20 minutes, lid on. Do not use an aluminium pan. After the mixture has cooled, fill glass jars, making sure the mushrooms are covered with liquid and a tight top. Keep in a cool place.

They are quite delicious eaten with cold meat, roast chicken and terrines. I export a few jars, to good friends only. One of them in Paris confessed to her self-indulgence. She had enjoyed this British offering on her own and on its own, as an *hors d'oeuvre*, with some crusty bread. I saw a sparkle in her eyes at the memory of the feast.

Les Crêpes

LES CRÊPES
Pancakes

Flambées, soufflées, with kirsch or Suzette, crêpes can bring a sophisticated finish to the evening. Yet for me the most memorable ones are very simple. Sprinkled with sugar, warm from the pan, they have a delicate, transparent edge that tells of lightness. They are just like the pancakes my mother used to make, working hard to keep up with the demands of the family; simple, happy memories that never fade or tarnish.

The origin of pancakes is modest and humble, dating back to the time when they were a bread substitute. The flour, or the base, could have been rye, wheat, buckwheat, maize, chestnut or even chick peas depending on the region. *Nicci*, in Corsica, *couqueback* in the North, *sauciaux* in Berry, *boulaigou* in Limousin, and so on. Each name keeps the flavour of its province, each tells of the main resources of the area. For better or for worse, wherever they come from and whatever the names, they are most welcome at the right time, and not too often. They are quick, easy, cheap and filling. With them, we keep in touch with our rural past and the early days of cooking. I have not forgotten these humble beginnings, since I read *Maria Chapdelaine*, a book on French Canada in the early days of the settlers. Life was rough and tough; the word gastronomy did not exist. Pancakes were the staple diet, made in bulk for the week — by the seventh day they were an unappetising mess, mouldy probably— a disturbing detail to my young imagination because pancakes are synonymous with pleasure and enjoyment. I heard a similar tale more recently about porridge made for the week and kept in a drawer (*plus ça change*). Pancakes have always enjoyed much popularity, at every level, whatever the age. Their versatility from ordinary to sophisticated is infinite.

Last century they gained their seal of notoriety or *lettres de noblesses* as crêpes Suzette. Everybody knows the story and the recipe. Both variations suit imagination and taste. Suzette, the pretty girl dining one night on the Riviera with the future Edward the VII became forever famous, courtesy of the prince. He insisted that the chef's creation be named after her. Some later version insists that there was no Suzette—Queen Victoria was there! The early version fits far better the century, the legend surrounding the prince and our romantic imagination.

In France pancakes are made traditionally for *Mardi Gras* (Shrove Tuesday) and *La Chandeleur* (Candlemas) on 2 February, when the church commemorates the Purification of the Virgin Mary. The faithful celebrated religiously with candles blessed in the church; it was symbolic of the arrival of Jesus, coinciding with the return of the longer days. At home, they made merry with pancakes and whatever drink was available locally—they are thirst-giving. The pancake celebration is thought to have been the idea of an early Pope, anxious to blot out from the people's minds the attraction of another pagan mid-February festival, licentious and popular.

The continuity of these simple traditions is like generations linking hands, reassuringly, year after year. Pancakes mean fun and fairs, but their religious origin is fading away. My father remembered village children going from farm to farm collecting eggs and flour to make pancakes. Nowadays, eggs are cheap and plentiful, and children have forgotten the custom.

Everybody seems to have their own recipe but the principle remains the same. For savoury pancakes add to the basic mixture grated nutmeg, chopped chives, finely chopped parsley, BEURRE NOISETTE brown butter (*beurre noisette*, butter cooked gently until it turns light brown, remembering though that it must not be too often if you are thinking of cholesterol and health). *Beurre noisette* can also be used for sweet pancakes for a rich flavour, with grated lemon or orange rind to give them a light pleasant taste, especially if the pancakes are eaten simply with a sprinkling of sugar and lemon juice *à l'anglaise*. Spread with home-made lemon curd, fruity and sharp, they are delicious—a treat, said French friends. Lemon curd—the real thing that is— would be a successful British export.

There are variations to the basic mixture.

1. With milk only they are tasty but heavy.
2. With water, what they lose in flavour they gain in texture. They are finer and crisper and they keep in the fridge or the deep freeze without having to be separated individually.
3. Half milk and half beer is another possibility—they are lighter in texture and supposedly more digestible.

4. Alcohol added to the batter gives a crisp pancake, finer and thinner.

5. For light, airy pancakes add a whisked white of egg to the batter, just before cooking. The basic mixture can be improved and the pancakes made more delicate with the addition of two yolks and extra fat.

6. As an extra refinement add cream—in moderation, otherwise they become soft and difficult to handle.

If yolks, cream and butter are added to the basic mixture, use less flour to get the same amount of pancakes. It gives a rich mixture and delicate pancakes—impossible to toss though. If the pancakes are needed without delay, add more eggs (2) and double the fat in the batter. No rest is required. To make a reasonable quantity of pancakes use two good quality frying pans. It speeds up the process. Occasionally, under pressure, I have used three pans at a time. It can be done, but I felt like a juggler in a hurry!

BASIC PANCAKE MIXTURE

Makes 2 dozen 20cm / 8 inch pancakes
250 g/9 oz sifted flour
3 medium to large eggs
Good pinch of salt (or 2 dsp sugar for sweet pancakes)
½ litre/18 fl oz water and/or milk
2 tbsp oil or melted butter

In a large bowl put the flour, the eggs, the oil (or melted butter), salt, or sugar for sweet pancakes, and mix. Add the liquid gradually, stirring carefully and thoroughly. Make sure there are no lumps in the batter, sieve if necessary or whisk in a machine. Cover the bowl and leave at room temperature for an hour at least—the pancakes will cook better without shrinking. More water is added then, until the consistency is right. The thinner the batter the lighter the pancake. My grandmother had a most unusual method—she would mix flour, eggs, flavouring and work it into a firm ball. After a couple of hours rest she added the liquid, a little at a time. A lot of work it seems, but her pancakes were always exceptionally thin and tasty.

143

Little fat is needed to make pancakes. With a good pan (non-stick is best) and oil or melted butter in the batter, it is not necessary, the first pancake excepted. In rural areas, a piece of back fat was rubbed over the frying pan—a quick, tidy operation. If fat is needed, use a potato cut in half, or cotton wool or cheesecloth, wrapped and tied over a fork and dipped in oil (or oil and melted butter). Rub the pan lightly in between pancakes. Check the fluidity of the pancakes and the temperature of the frying pan (medium hot). Both are essential for light pancakes and make it a lot easier. Pour a little batter from a small ladle, tilting the pan so that the mixture is evenly distributed. Pour any surplus back; soon it is easy to assess the right quantity. When the pancake begins to cook, it turns paler, shake the pan and when the pancake moves freely, turn it over with a spatula, or toss it; the finer the pancake the more difficult it is to toss. Children love giving a hand at this stage—the simple magic of pancakes! To keep the pancakes warm, pile them up on a plate sitting on a pan of hot water, with a second plate on top.

At Candlemas grandmothers would dream a little, tossing a pancake with one hand whilst holding a gold coin in the other. If the toss was successful, it meant prosperity all the year round! Talking to an older friend about this custom, she giggled and said, 'Every year, gold coin in hand, I toss *my* pancake'. *Joie de vivre* and optimism rang in her voice.

MATEFAIM
A Tasty, Filling Pancake

I sampled this thick pancake, a *farinade*, in a little village of Aveyron; it was simple, good and substantial. Afterwards we

ate grilled local lamb served piping hot on a bed of wild thyme from the hills. It was perfect, full of flavour and aroma. And thyme, of course, like many aromatic herbs, helps digestion. These thick pancakes, by the way, are served flat or folded, not rolled like the thinner ones.

Basic mixture for *Matefaim*

125 g/4½ oz flour

3 eggs (medium sized)
250 ml/9 fl.oz water
Salt, pepper
100 g/4 oz streaky bacon cut thick
1 tbsp chopped herbs, chives, parsley etc
2 tbsp oil for frying

Make the batter. Rest for one hour if possible. Before cooking, add the herbs, grill or parboil the streaky bacon, chop and add to the batter. If grilled, mix the fat with the batter which should be thickish but fluid. For *matefaims* use a pan with a thick base (20 cm/8 ins diameter). Warm up the oil, and when it is hot, add the mixture—lower the heat after a minute or so, cover and cook for 5 or 6 minutes. Turn onto the other side and cook for the same length of time. Alternatively, finish cooking under the grill. Cut into wedges, (a good 15 cm thick), eat warm or hot. In the south-west the wheat flour is sometimes replaced by finely ground maize.

A *matefaim* flavoured with onions or herbs is a good accompaniment for ham, sliced boiled gammon, or well-seasoned cottage cheese. Without the bacon it is ideal for meat-less days, quick, economical and far better than instant food and its additives. It takes a few minutes to prepare the batter: do it hours ahead if necessary. The rest of the meal is quickly put together, including a salad. Any light crisp green mixture is good. Recently with a *matefaim* we had a raw spinach salad. SPINACH AND Mix with a sharp, peppery vinaigrette half an hour before bring- WALNUT SALAD ing to the table. The spinach becomes limp, add chopped walnuts, one can buy them shelled quite easily. If they are no longer fresh (the oil in them oxidises rather quickly and becomes rancid) soak them in salted water for at least three hours. They come out refreshed and pleasant, although I am not too sure of the chemistry involved! A wonderful pancake filling is walnut and creamed stilton, so it is worth taking such trouble.

This thick pancake batter can be enriched with cottage cheese (100 g/4 oz), quark or soft goat cheese, if available. Stilton or Roquefort, crumbled and softened with a little cream, would also do. Thick pancakes turn easily into hearty puddings by adding fruit to the batter.

145

CRÊPES RUSTIQUES
Traditional Country Pancake

For 6 to 8 pancakes
Basic mixture for Matefaim
80 g/2 tbsp sugar
500 g/1 lb apples
2 tbsp alcohol—brandy, Calvados, or malt whisky
Oil or butter for frying

Prepare the batter as in previous recipe for *matefaim*, add half the sugar and let it rest. Peel and slice the apples finely, sprinkle with the rest of the sugar and the chosen alcohol. Add the fruit mixture to the batter before cooking. Warm up the oil and/or butter, pour in a ladleful of fruity batter. Cook slowly to soften the fruit, cover with a lid. Turn over and finish cooking. Replace the apples with pears, or bananas (using brown sugar and rum), mixed fruit, or tinned exotic fruit, a taste of honey, grated lemon rind, fresh ginger, the variations are legion. In season, make a thick pancake with one pound of stoned cherries. Flavour with Kirsch, if available. It is a rustic ancestor of the much lighter and creamier *clafoutis*.

CHERRY
PANCAKE

If you choose to make a single thick pancake in a big enough frying pan, enough to feed everyone, grease the pan more generously and cook for a longer period. In this case it really is easier to finish cooking under the grill, especially when adding egg whites.

Sprinkle with icing sugar and caramelise under the hot grill. It gives it a nice finish. In my part of France, those simple puddings were quite often flambé, with local fiery *eau de vie*; it had an almost magic effect at the dinner table. Remember that all the alcohol burns away , leaving a very aromatic flavour.

For fine savoury pancakes, follow the basic recipe adapting it to your needs. There is an infinite variety of fillings, some more traditional than others. With a little imagination there are plenty of tasty combinations. Moreover, it is an easy and quite elegant way of using left-over chicken, fish, ham, mushrooms, cheese, sweetbreads etc.

146 Once prepared the batter can wait for a few hours, or the

pancakes can be cooked ahead, wrapped and kept in a cool place (or even a freezer for longer planning or unexpected visitors). Here are a few traditional recipes

FICELLES PICARDES
A Speciality from Picardy

For 6 pancakes
Basic pancake mixture
Ham, 1 slice per person
125 g/4 oz mushrooms
1 dsp cream
A touch of finely-grated nutmeg
A little tarragon to taste
Cheese 80 gm/3 oz—Gruyère and Parmesan, Emmenthal or
  Gouda
Salt, freshly ground pepper
Béchamel sauce: 25 g/3oz butter
                25 g/1oz flour
                300 ml/10 fl.oz milk

Fill the pancakes with a mixture of well-flavoured Béchamel sauce, mixed with the cream, nutmeg, ham and mushrooms, lightly sautéed in a little butter and lemon juice. Lay one fine slice of ham on each filled pancake, roll them up like cigars then lay them tightly side by side in an oven dish, sprinkle with grated cheese—Gruyère and Parmesan or Emmenthal or Gouda. Dot with butter and brown them under the grill. It is very tasty and filling. Two pancakes each and a green salad make a satisfying main course.

CRÊPES AUX FRUITS DE MER
Pancakes with Seafood

Shrimps, prawns, mussels, fish (monkfish is very good), small scallops, clams (a tin will do) turn an ordinary pancake into a gastronomic delight. It is always better to select at least three from this list for mixing flavours and textures.

For 6 to 8 pancakes
300 g/10 oz seafood

150 g/5 oz cooked fish
2 shallots
2 egg yolks
100 ml/4 fl.oz or small glass of white wine
1 tbsp cream
Clam juice (if available)
1 tsp flour
Oil and butter for cooking

Fry the finely chopped shallots, sprinkle with the flour. Add clam juice and wine. Cook gently, add the seafood and season. When it is hot, mix in the yolks with the cream—stop cooking at this stage.

Fill the pancakes, fold twice or roll. Glaze under a hot grill spreading them first with a spoonful of cream. In France these seafood pancakes can be bought at a good *Charcutier* or *Traiteur* at the weekend, good enough for Sunday lunches and *jours de fête* (special days), when mother needs a break.

CRÊPES AU SAUMON ET À L'OSEILLE
Salmon and Sorrel Pancake

A little left-over salmon with a creamy sorrel sauce makes a delicious filling and goes a long way. Use an enriched batter for the pancakes.

Basic pancake mixture
250 g/½ lb cooked salmon
1 dsp cream
1 yolk of egg
100 g/4 oz sorrel

Cook the sorrel briefly in a little butter, stir in the cream and a yolk. Mix together with the fish, fill the pancakes and glaze under a hot grill with cream or serve straight away. Alternatively DILL AND the salmon could be mixed with a creamy dill sauce and small CUCUMBER cubes of poached cucumber: it is light and nicely flavoured.

RATATOUILLE For a vegetarian touch, fill the pancakes with ratatouille (a left-PANCAKES over, maybe, well reheated until the texture is soft and creamy). 148 Check the seasoning. Fold or roll. Cover with fine slices of cheese, melt under the grill or in the oven. Season with freshly ground black pepper.

GÂTEAUX DE CRÊPES AUX ASPERGES
Asparagus Pancake Cake

For 12 pancakes
Basic pancake mixture
Juice of 1 lemon
2 egg yolks
250 g/½ lb cooked asparagus or two tins, sliced
Béchamel sauce
1 tbsp thick cream
Seasoning

Make Béchamel sauce using some reduced liquid from the asparagus to replace some of the milk. Add the cream. Mix the asparagus into the sauce with the yolks and lemon juice. Heat but do not boil. Season. Spread each pancake with some of the asparagus Béchamel, pile them one on top of the other to make a cake. Sprinkle with grated cheese or cover with the rest of the Béchamel mixed with grated cheese and brown in the oven. Reheat if necessary but do not overcook. Cover with foil first. A similar cake can be made with cooked spinach, Béchamel and a smooth cottage cheese.

SWEET PANCAKES

For thin pancakes, use the basic recipe (if necessary adjusting the quantities) adding sugar and flavouring. For special occassions and special fillings add yolks, butter or cream to the batter.

CRÊPES AUX POMMES
Apple Pancakes

500 g/1 lb eating apples
100 g/4 oz sugar
100 g/4 oz butter

Peel and slice the apples, cook in a frying pan with the butter. When the apples begin to soften and colour, add the sugar. 149

Lower the heat and cover for a couple of minutes. That way the apples will soften completely without requiring more butter or sugar. As soon as the sugary mixture begins to colour, watch carefully and remove the moment it dries up or colours a little. Spread some on each pancake, roll or fold twice. Ordinary stewed apples can be used and the flavour boosted with vanilla, honey, cinnamon, cider or lemon rind. Arrange on a plate, keep warm until pudding time, in the oven, protected with aluminium foil. Warm a glass of brandy or malt whisky, apple or pear brandy; light and pour on the hot pancakes.

CRÊPES AUX BANANES SAUTÉES
Fried Bananas and Pancakes

For 6 pancakes
Basic pancake mixture
1 banana per person
50 g/2 oz butter (or butter and oil)
1 heaped dsp sugar
1 tbsp rum

Fry the banana in butter and oil (or just butter); the heat must not be too brisk. The banana softens and colours. Add the sugar and caramelise. Roll each banana in a pancake, sprinkle with icing sugar or flambé with rum. The easiest way is to warm up the rum (or brandy) in a little pan (if it is brass and decorative all the better) then light. Bananas of course could be sliced before cooking.

  Fried bananas sprinkled with freshly ground pepper, wrapped in a thin slice of ham and then in a pancake, make a tasty and easy dish. It would be fun for a child to prepare (and eat!). Arrange in an oven dish (tightly), sprinkle with grated cheese (Emmenthal, Gouda or Fontina) and serve with a salad (lettuce and orange, for example, sharpened with lemon juice).

CRÊPES MARTINIQUE

For 4 people
Basic pancake mixture
3 large bananas, finely sliced

125 ml/4 fl.oz water
75 g/3 oz sugar
$\frac{1}{2}$ cinnamon stick
2 dsp sultanas, soaked in rum

Boil together the water and sugar to make a syrup which should not be too thick. Infuse the cinnamon in the syrup, boil gently for 10 to 15 minutes, sieve into another pan, add the bananas and poach until soft. The mixture should not now be runny. Fill the pancakes (before the beginning of the meal if necessary) and keep warm. Make 1 pint of vanilla ice-cream (or buy good quality ice-cream), soften it a little and add a good handful of sultanas that have been soaked in rum for an hour. Freeze again. Serve the banana pancakes with the ice-cream. They are simple, but spicey and succulent.

CRÊPES À LA CRÈME PATISSIÈRE
Pastry Cream Pancakes

The *pastry cream* can be flavoured with vanilla, coffee, praline (burnt almond) kirsch for example; the choices are endless. Make smaller pancakes for this recipe, about 15 cm/6 ins.

Basic pancake mixture
$\frac{1}{2}$ litre/17 fl. oz milk
4 egg yolks
80 g/2 tbsp sugar
60 g/2 oz flour or $\frac{1}{2}$ and $\frac{1}{2}$ flour and cornflour
Cointreau or Kirsch (optional)

Whisk the sugar and the yolks, add the flour diluted with a few tablespoons of cold milk. Boil the rest of the milk and add to the mixture little by little. Cook, stirring all the time; take off the heat when it begins to bubble. Cool, add Cointreau or Kirsch if you wish. Because of the added flour, this is much easier to make than egg custard.

SOUFFLÉ PANCAKES

For delicate and soft pancakes simply whisk the whites of 4 eggs until stiff and mix into the pastry cream. The recipe with proper timing can be done successfully and without effort. Prepare the 151 pancakes and the pastry cream beforehand. Preheat the oven (200C/400F/mark 6) during the meal: whisk the whites and add to the custard at the last minute. In an ovenproof dish arrange the pancakes. Put 2 tablespoons of the soufflé mixture in one half, fold the other half loosely over it. Sprinkle with icing sugar, cook for 6 to 7 minutes in the oven, serve straight away.

A thick fruit purée and a little *pastry cream* is another possibility for a filling, though more unusual, and even nicer. Serve the pancakes with a cool, smooth fruit sauce, not too sweet, using the same fruit or a different one to enhance, contrast or accentuate the flavour. For example, apples with pear sauce; pears with red currant sauce; strawberry purée with rasberry sauce, flavoured with orange juice or a little Cointreau. Smooth apricot jam can be added to the custard but in this case reduce the sugar in the recipe and flambé the pancake.

CRÊPES AU CAFÉ
Coffee Pancakes

For 12 pancakes
Basic pancake recipe
½ litre/18 fl.oz milk
50 g/2 oz coffee beans, coarsely ground
100 g/4 oz unsalted butter

Infuse the coffee beans in hot milk and simmer gently for a few minutes. Strain it and use for making the pastry cream (see pastry cream pancakes). While the pastry cream is still warm, add the butter, whisking in a little at a time. It is tasty and delicately smooth and glossy. Spread each pancake with a little of the custard (keep some for the top). Keep them flat and pile them one on top of the other.

For variation, take some shelled walnuts (make sure the taste is fresh), add one spoonful of sugar and grind coarsely together. Add to the last of the coffee custard. Cover the top with it and decorate with walnut halves. For another contrast of flavours and colours melt 100 g/4 oz good chocolate with a little water, mix with 1 spoonful double cream and spread over the top. A sprinkling of slivered almonds (toasted) gives an alternative finish with a crunch. The cake is rich and well flavoured.

Curacao and tangerine were probably used in the original recipe. Any orange liqueur like Grand Marnier or Cointreau is a good alternative. Many people enjoy the flavour of orange juice, sharpened with lemon juice and grated orange peel. Personally, I like the taste of tangerine; the aroma is quite unique.

For 4 people
8 pancakes (thin and delicate) 15 cm/6 ins
100 g/4 oz butter
8 oz sugar lumps
1 orange or 2 tangerines
2 tbsp of Curacao (to taste)
1 liqueur glass of brandy

Cream the butter, rub the sugar lumps over the tangerines or oranges until they colour and are well soaked with the aromatic essence or use the finely grated peel. Mix the flavoured sugar lumps with the butter until creamy, add gradually the orange juice (as if making rum butter) and the Curacao. Spread the pancakes with this flavoured butter, fold twice and lay in a hot serving dish (keep warm in the oven, protected with aluminium foil). Bring to the table, pour the warmed brandy and light, tilting the dish slightly to make sure all the alcohol burns away. It is easy, tastes superb and brings happy smiles all round.

DINÉR AUX CRÊPES
A Pancake Party

It is fun: make plenty of pancakes ahead—guests will help themselves to the fillings. Fruit juices, cider or light white wine are pleasantly thirst-quenching for such a feast. Here are some suggestions for fillings:

1. Hot frankfurters and mustard.
2. Creamy, lightly-cooked scrambled eggs mixed with smoked salmon (left-over trimmings are ideal) kept warm over hot water; or potted shrimps, very British and most enjoyable.
3. Béchamel sauce with ham (or chicken) flavoured with tarragon and chives.
4. Cheesy Béchamel with a little cayenne (using farm cheddar, 153

Brie or Edam).
5.   Creamed smoked haddock; creamy spinach; Ratatouille.

Once you get the idea, think up fillings of your own. Provide bowls of finely chopped parsley and chives and a large green salad.

The sweet fillings can vary from very simple to elaborate and can be hot or cold. All the following go well with pancakes:

1.   Good jam: home-made with cherry or apricot; honey and newly-made marmalade.
2.   Home-made lemon or orange curd.
3.   Bowls of cream and pastry cream, the latter flavoured to taste, as in previous recipes.
4.   Small jugs of freshly squeezed lemon and orange juice.
5.   Bowls of various sugars, both brown and white.
6.   Small jugs of liqueurs such as Kirsch, malt whisky and Curacao.

Lay the bowls and jugs on a large table covered with a colourful checked cloth, French style. This is an ideal party for a big country kitchen, almost like a do-it-yourself feast. With a little encouragement and no doubt great gusto, guests, male or female, will help to make more pancakes whenever required. Do not be too ambitious though, limit your numbers to ten or twelve relaxed and enthusiastic friends.

Oranges du Soleil

ORANGES DU SOLEIL
Sunkissed Oranges

Oranges are at their best, sweet and juicy, in the middle of winter. Navel oranges make delicious salads or garnishes. First peeled to the quick, *à vif*, they easily come out in quarters, minus the fine membrane. Flavoured with a little orange liqueur, or a little orange blossom water, they are fragrant. sophisticated and always appreciated.

Herb teas are gaining ground in Britain, some nicely scented like verbena, or definitely fragrant like mint. Special concoctions may be effective cures for specific problems, but like real old fashioned medicines they often taste vile. A drink made with warm water (or milk) flavoured with a little orange blossom water, sweetened with orange blossom honey is pleasant, delicately scented and soothing. The pretty coloured bottles sold in France at the chemist, herbalist or reliable *épiceries fines* (delicatessens), are concentrated and excellent; only a little is needed. The year of harvesting (they pick the buds one by one to extract the aroma) should be mentioned, a guarantee of quality.

ORANGE BLOSSOM TEA

From my school days I remember another version of orange salad, sliced but unpeeled and marinaded in sweet white wine. It certainly looked attractive and had its followers. As for me, I remember removing the peel, slowly, laboriously, with patience and my spoon. We ate it on 25 November when we celebrated St Catherine, patron saint of students and twenty-five year old unmarried girls. We, the schoolgirls, ranged between ten and nineteen. The teaching staff, presided over by the head on that occasion, ate with us at a table in the middle of the refectory—a real *glass bowl*. Some of the younger teachers arrived with fancy head gear on, a tradition when you were a *Catherinette*. Anyway the dinner was delicious and everybody, the girls at least, looked forward to the feast.

Moroccan oranges and clementines from Corsica mixed with bright green leaves (their trade mark) are displayed outside the shops to tempt passers-by. On a wet miserable December day, in Scotland, these cheerful messengers of the sun look out of place but they are full of memories. In Corsica, I saw them 157 growing between the hills and the sea. In early November they were still a little green, a little tart. A few weeks later, miles away from *l'Île de Beauté*, the sweetness is perfect. A bowl filled with sunny clementines, or the fragrance of a leaf rubbed between my fingers, never fails to cheer me up when skies are low and grey. Holiday breakfasts in Spain with freshly squeezed orange, freshly made hot *churros* and coffee are the ideal start to a relaxed day. A Spaniard would prefer *churros* with a cup of hot creamy chocolate—*à chacun son goût*.

A cool refreshing drink with fresh orange juice and a little port is delicious: 1 tablespoon of port to each glass of freshly squeezed juice with a little sugar added. It is hardly alcoholic but nicely different. Serve it cool, with ice-cubes in summer.

Orange slices, marinated in brandy for a few hours, make a pleasant addition to a glass of white wine.

ORANGE À L'ARMAGNAC
Orange with Armagnac

In student days, under the expert guidance of a Gascon friend, I tried a speciality from his area, *orange à l'armagnac à la Gersoise*. By the fire on a winter evening it dispelled a touch of gentle melancholy, *vague à l'âme*, in no time and so very pleasantly.

1 orange per person, medium-sized and juicy
Sugar to taste
1 wine glass Armagnac per person

It is important that the oranges are of a reasonable size so as to keep a clear head to the end of the tasting. Cut a third off the top. Sprinkle with a little sugar and a little Armagnac. With a teaspoon, scoop out a little of the inside and enjoy the combination. As you proceed, refuel with a little more Armagnac and a little more sugar as the orange becomes more and more hollow, but beware of excesses! Malt whisky would be excellent too, and it would become orange *à l'écossaise*.

CAFÉ BRÛLOT

An unusual way to drink coffee with an orange flavour is *café brûlot*. It is a change from Gaelic coffee with whisky and cream or black coffee flavoured with cardamom. It is easy to prepare and will create a warm atmosphere after dinner with convivial company. It is *brûlot* because of the burnt brandy added to it.

1 cup of strong coffee per person, sweetened to taste
The rind of 1 orange
1 clove (optional)
½ cinnamon stick (for four) broken into pieces to release more aroma
1 liqueur glass brandy per person

At the start of the meal put brandy, peel and spices together in a small pan to develop and blend the flavours. Make the coffee as usual. Heat, but do not boil, the brandy mixture. Light with a match and swirl the pan gently (at the table if you like a touch of showmanship). Pour the hot coffee onto the brandy while it is still alight—or when the flames have died down, if alcohol does not suit. Serve very hot in previously warmed cups.

Some twenty years ago I brought back from France some old-fashioned coffee cups, *Mazagrans*. Tulip shaped, they fit nicely and warmly in one's hand. Nowadays they are made once again in French potteries and can be found there in certain china shops.

Originally *brûlot* was simply a lump of sugar soaked in a teaspoon filled with *eau-de-vie*, lit and then added slowly to the coffee. My husband reminds me that, in past centuries, *brûlots* were the fireships that the French unleashed upon unsuspecting enemies.

Citrus peels add a warm, fruity aroma to *sangria*, mulled wine or punch. One of my early delights in an old *Larousse Gastronomique*, though orange is not included, was the making of a giant grog. It makes a fascinating after dinner story.

On the 25th October 1599, Sir Edward Kennel, Commander-in-Chief of the British Naval Forces, offered a gigantic punch to his assembled crews, which was prepared in a huge marble fountain in the centre of his estate. To make it, the following materials were employed: 80 casks of *eau de vie*, 90 casks of distilled water, 25,000 large limes, 80 pints of lemon juice, 13 quintals (1 quintal = 100 kg) of Lisbon sugar, 5 pounds of nutmeg and 1 huge cask of Malaga wine.

A canopy had been erected over the fountain to protect it
from the rain and the service was carried out by a cabin boy
who rowed in this sea of punch in a tiny boat made of rosewood.
In order to serve the 6,000 guests it was necessary to change
the cabin boys several times, as they became intoxicated with
the fumes from this sea of alcohol within a quarter of an hour!

One Saturday afternoon in midwinter I went shopping with
my son. At the greengrocer I noticed that some of my favourite
oranges had just arrived and I asked for 'ten bloody oranges,
please'. My son whispered in my ear, 'You know they are really
called blood oranges'. My word for word translation was wrong
and had been wrong for quite a long time! On my next visit
to the greengrocer to buy more *oranges sanguines*, I reproached
him gently for saying nothing all these years. As he handed me
the fruit he said, grinning, 'Och, it's alright, Mrs Murray. Here
are your bloody oranges!'.

I keep buying them, year after year; they are sweet, juicy and
different. My mother had a special liking for them, cutting them
open and delighting, like a child, in their colouring. The darker
they were the more exciting it was. They make attractive salads
and add a lovely tinge to a mayonnaise, or Hollandaise sauce.
Nowadays we take oranges for granted, and yet they only grow
in warm, sunny places where the winters are short and mild.
Originally they came from India for the Seville type, and China
for the sweet ones. In previous centuries, because of their
novelty, they had great appeal, the appeal of the exotic and rare.

In the early 17th Century, Henri IV, King of France, gave
orders for an *orangerie* to be set up in the Thuileries (as it was
spelt then) in Paris. (It is now a museum.) Later, Louis XIV,
Henri's grandson, had his own *orangerie* at Versailles, designed
by Mansart, his architect. Soon, royal visitors came to admire
the oranges in their elegant showcase. Come winter and its
mists, these exiles from the sun found some consolation, maybe,
in the royal visits of the *Roi Soleil* and his ladies. Nothing was
more pleasing to the ladies than a royal gift of an orange. In
England, Charles II's delight in Nell Gwynn and her oranges
drew the same exotic parallel.

The day I picked my first orange, in Portugal, was a childhood dream come true. At a wedding we went to there the bride
wore orange blossom in her hair, newly picked from the

garden—a most romantic touch. The most heavenly memory of all was the fragrance of orange blossom—*el azahar*—one night above Valencia. The Arabian nights living on . . .

CRÈME À L'ORANGE
Orange Pudding

This is light and refreshing and Nordic in origin. In Germany it was served with whipped cream and a light, lemony egg custard and made with red berries.

For 4 to 5 people
5 -6 juicy oranges
Juice of 1 lemon
Grated rind of 1 orange
150 g/5 oz sugar according to taste and the sweetness of the fruit
80 g/3 oz cornflour or arrowroot
1 liqueur glass Cointreau or Curacao (optional)
1 or 2 whites of egg (optional)

Squeeze the oranges and the lemon, and add the finely grated rind. Add the sugar and, if necessary, some water to make up to $\frac{3}{4}$ litre/27 fl.oz. Heat in a pan (not aluminium), add cornflour or arrowroot diluted with a little cold water. Bring gently to the boil, stirring continuously. As soon as the mixture thickens, take it off the heat and, if wished, add stiffly beaten egg whites while hot. This makes the pudding lighter. Mix in the orange liqueur and pour into a jelly mould, rinsed but not dried. Leave in the fridge (or a cool place) until set. Before turning it out onto a flat shallow serving dish, rinse the mould under the tap to help position the pudding more easily. Alternatively, make individual puddings. Serve with whipped cream. The recipe is easy and simple and there are many possibilities and pleasant combinations for those who like change and variety. It is usually made with soft fruits such as red-currants, raspberries, cranberries or blueberries.

Here are a few ideas to decorate.

Fine strips of orange peel, cut thinly and regularly, first parboiled and then cooked in a syrup (50/50 mixture of sugar and water) until it thickens. Or serve with whole peeled clementines poached in a light syrup flavoured with vanilla or liqueur. This adds sophistication and freshness.

Contrast the colour and flavour with half strawberries, sliced kiwis or black grapes, peeled, stoned and halved. To serve more people, add an exotic fruit salad: bananas, pineapple and pink grapefruit, flavoured with orange flower water.

Orange (sweet or bitter) or tangerine peel, dried in a cool oven and kept in an airtight jar, is useful at any time for milk puddings or sauces, always a way in grandmother's day of conjuring up the inimitable flavour of oranges whatever the season. These peels, like garlands, used to dry inside the huge fire places of the old farm houses. If you have them in excess, they make good fire kindling! Earlier in the season, stalks from field mushrooms were dried in the hot sun. They were threaded beforehand for ease and convenience. I remember doing that job, as a little girl, well pleased with the responsibility.

In Meg Dod's Scottish cookery book, I found a list with a date, written with application by the resident cook of the day, presumably the last one to use the book. It was a link across the years, an interest and pleasure, bridging over generations and nationalities. The length and complexity of some of the recipes needed much enthusiasm, dedication and stamina. There was a chapter on Franco–English cuisine that particularly interested me. In it were several recipes from Carème, the high priest of *nouvelle cuisine* in the 18th century. He improved cooking greatly and gave it a new impetus, spreading the good word in many European courts as a chef. Here is one of his recipes, adapted to suit our modern circumstances.

ORANGES EN GELÉE
Jellied Oranges

For 4 people
5 — 6 medium-sized oranges
1 lemon (or tangerine)
1 oz or 7 leaves gelatine (enough for 1 pint)
1 glass orange liqueur (Cointreau or Curacao)
Rind of 1 orange
Sugar to taste

Choose 4 well shaped oranges with a deep colour. Cut a piece SUNKISSED ORANGES off the stalk end. With a teaspoon, raise the rind and empty the oranges. Put the orange skins in a bowl of cold water to toughen and plump up. Liquidise the fruit and sieve, or use a *mouli-légume*. Mix with the lemon juice (or tangerine), add Cointreau or Curacao, the finely grated rind of one orange and a little syrup. The quantity and strength of the syrup depends on the juice obtained. Around 150 ml is required for an average sized orange. Warm the juice slightly, dissolve the gelatine and mix in a little at a time to the warmed syrup. If the skin of any of the oranges break, a little butter will cover over the cracks perfectly (a useful tip!). Place the orange skins on a flat dish and pour in the mixture. Keep in a cold place until set. Serve individually on a plain or crystal plate. The oranges will stand perfectly, provided a little skin is cut off at the base before filling.

Many colourful or tasty touches can be added. Serve with orange sablés (dipped at one end in chocolate, optional), or *orangettes* (glacéed orange peel, cut into slices 1 cm wide, dipped ORANGETTES in good chocolate melted with a little butter, and dried on an oiled cake rack). Decorate simply with a few green leaves (clementine leaves in season or fresh bay leaves). Angelica, cut into strips, is another attractive touch, with or without whipped cream flavoured with orange liqueur.

This recipe from Carème is an old fashioned and attractive way to make and present orange jelly—pretty and delicate. Nowadays it would be more likely to make jelly in a mould or *nouvelle cuisine* style in a rectangular dish , adding perhaps, peeled pink grapefruit or orange segments while the jelly is set-ting. Decorate with half strawberries flavoured with orange liqueur or peeled lychees sliced and arranged around the dish. Serve with a smooth raspberry or strawberry *coulis* (fruit puréed FRUIT COULIS with the juice of a lemon to sharpen and accentuate the flavour, sweetened to taste).

RIZ AU LAIT
Rice Pudding French Style

From my early days at the village school, one incident has remained very clearly in my memory down to the boy's very 163 name. A senior, thirteen or so, created a stir one lunchtime when pudding was being served. The noisy room became quiet and a rumour went along the benches from one table to the other, *Fanfelle does not like rice pudding.* The war restrictions were coming to an end and the thought of unwanted *riz au lait* was simply unbelievable. I now have more extensive, sophisticated or expensive tastes, but now and then there is suddenly a need for simple *riz au lait*! This tasty, old fashioned recipe, popular with all and very adaptable is more like a cake than a pudding.

For 6 people
200 g/7 oz pudding rice
¾ litre/1 1/4 pints milk
100 g/4 oz sugar
3 large eggs
50 g/2 oz unsalted butter (plus some for the mould)
1 thin piece of orange peel, dried or fresh
100 g/4 oz fine strips of glacé orange peel

Wash the rice and cook for a good five minutes in plenty of boiling water, to soften it. Drain and add to the hot milk, infused with the peel with sugar added. Use a pyrex dish with a tight lid. Cook in the oven for 30 minutes or so at a low heat (160c/ 325F/mark 3). The rice should be soft, fluffy and ready for the last stage. Cool a little, add the chopped glacé peel, the butter cut into pieces and the beaten eggs, mix thoroughly. Butter a baking dish—for a nice effect use the fluted type used to make brioche. The rice being already cooked and the mixture warm, the pudding sets quickly in a warm oven (20 to 30 minutes). Cool for 5 to 10 minutes, loosen the sides with a knife and turn onto a flat or shallow dish. Serve warm or cold, cutting portions like a cake. For a lighter pudding, whisk the white of egg beforehand and stir into the mixture before the last stage.

CARAMEL If a caramel coating is chosen, no butter is needed for the baking dish. For the caramel melt 100 g/4 oz sugar with 2 tablespoons water. Heat, and when the caramel is just colouring, pour into the mould and coat evenly by tilting the dish around.

With orange flavoured rice (or tangerine or lemon), a fruity sauce enhances the flavour. Tangerines poached in a light vanilla syrup make the pudding more refreshing and sophisticated. A liqueur glass of orange or mandarin liqueur added to the fruit enhances the flavour even further. More simply, one or two SUNKISSED ORANGES small juicy oranges cut into slices and poached in syrup are decorative and fragrant, arranged all around the rice.

An apricot and orange sauce is quick; the mixed flavours APRICOT AND ORANGE SAUCE combine well. Warm up 3 to 4 tablespoons of good quality apricot jam (sieved or puréed), the juice of one or two oranges and thicken with a little arrowroot or cornflour, if necessary. An egg custard, flavoured with grated peel, liqueur or orange water, is a more classical accompaniment for rice pudding. In the south of France, simple and traditional puddings often required flavouring with orange water, a legacy from the Arabs. I am not too sure that I liked it as a child. Nowadays I am more partial to it but it is difficult to find in this country. These are only a few suggestions, a few ideas, mixing the cooking of the past and present.

ORANGE FLAVOURING MADE WITH VODKA AND ORANGE PEEL

Fill a small jar with fine strips of orange peel; cover with vodka (flavourless) and close the jar tightly. After a week or two, strain the extract into small bottles with screw tops. Use whenever required. A teaspoon may be enough to give a lift to almost any orange dish, savoury or sweet, requiring extra sharpness. Lemon peel, or a vanilla pod, cut into pieces and split, give good VANILLA AND LEMON EXTRACT extracts made the same way. They are useful when a lemon or vanilla flavour is required and make nice little presents.

The regime in French boarding schools has always been gentler than in their British equivalents. Every Thursday there was a holiday in my schooldays. Outings were allowed from 2 to 4pm before return to studies. On the way back to school there was a compulsory stop at the *pâtisserie*. The choice was great, my selection always wavered between the same favourites, round plump *noix japonaises*, concealing under their smooth chocolate JAPONAISES coating a round *chou* bun filled generously with chocolate butter cream, smooth and velvety. It melted slowly and deliciously in the mouth, sweetening the return to school. Or there were the coffee éclairs, well flavoured with coffee pastry cream inside and ÉCLAIRS coffee icing outside, smooth and glossy and perfect. The chocolate éclairs in a line beside them offered another alternative. Bland sweet whipped cream is a much poorer filling than pastry cream.

In May came peaches as seen by the *pâtissier's* eyes—two halves like mini-brioches lightly soaked in Kirsch, and bound together with a delicate butter cream. A little of the cream was kept and coloured to make a pale green leaf. A sugary blush on each cheek gave the artist's finishing touch and a most irresistible look that alone would help to sell many. Last, but not least, were the rum-babas—lighter and less cloying than cream cakes. The rum syrup, fragrant, cool and refreshing, was a favourite on hot days.

The idea of moistening the *kugelhof* (cake made with yeast and sultanas) with rum is very regal. It is said that the exiled Polish King Stanislas (Louis XV's father-in-law) enjoyed cooking as much as eating. Finding the cake too dry for his liking, he sprinkled it with rum. Having tried *kugelhof* in Alsace, I rather approve of the idea—a successful inspiration that in time spread all over France. Rum is no longer used neat (temperance and economy!) but highly diluted in a syrup and still very aromatic. *Babas* or *savarins* (the larger version) made in special crown-like moulds, need yeast, time and patience.

In Britain I make a light cake moistened with an orange syrup. This idea came out of a French recipe book by Mapie de Toulouse Lautrec; my first cookery book, at a time when I knew what I wanted, but not necessarily how to do it. Nowadays there are many similar recipes, with port, white wine and other flavourings.

Prepare a sponge cake, or light madeira cake flavoured with orange. When it is ready and still hot, moisten generously with orange and brandy or whisky, rum or port syrup. It turns into a delicious sponge.

GATEAU À L'ORANGE
Orange Cake

100 g/4 oz caster sugar
100 g/4 oz flour
50 g/2 oz cornflour
Grated peel of 1 orange

3 dsp oil or melted butter
1 tsp baking powder (optional)
4 large eggs

Separate the eggs. Whisk the yolks and sugar until white and foamy. Add flour, peel, baking powder and oil. Whisk the whites until stiff, adding a pinch of salt or a little lemon juice. Mix a tablespoonful with the batter then add the rest, gently lifting to keep the air in. Butter a cake tin and cook in a warm oven (180c/350F/mark 4) for 30 to 35 minutes. Before taking the cake out check that it is ready, using a knitting needle which should come out dry. Leave in the oven, switched off, door ajar, for a few minutes.

SIROP À L'ORANGE
Orange Syrup

Juice of 6 oranges
Peel of 1 orange
2 tbsp sugar
1 small glass of orange liqueur or rum

While the cake is baking, make the syrup. To be on the safe side, make plenty, a good ½ litre (almost a pint). Mix the orange juice, rind and sugar together until the sugar has melted completely. Do not boil. Add the chosen alcohol last to the cooled syrup.

Soak the cake well while it is hot but leave a little of the syrup aside. Warm up and sieve 3 tablespoons of apricot jam to coat the cake with (orange and apricot go well together, although this is optional). Use the rest of the syrup to freshen up the cake before serving very cold. I was reminded of that important detail by a tiny boy (four or five, maybe) as he and his father waited for their turn at the *pâtisserie*. As soon as the rum-babas were ordered, the child came closer to the counter and said anxiously to the assistant, *et surtout bien arrosés*—and above all, well soaked. With a sprinkler and a large smile she gave the cakes an extra ration.

Accompany the cake with whipped cream, made lighter by adding one or two egg whites, whisked stiffly, or serve with a cool egg custard (flavoured with liqueur or orange peel).

CRÈME À LA PURÉE D'ORANGE
Baked Orange Custard

Wipe the orange with a little malt vinegar, then rinse and keep in cold water for the night. Blanch for a few minutes. This operation is repeated twice, changing the water each time—it removes some of the bitterness.

Liquidise the whole orange in a mixer, or purée in an old fashioned *mouli-légumes*. Mix with one tablespoon of flour and one small glass of rum or cointreau. Add to a baked custard mixture and cook in a warm oven. It gives a different character to a traditional pudding. Bake as usual, turn onto a dish, cool and serve with a chocolate sauce made from good chocolate. It is undoubtedly more expensive but it contains more cocoa (around 50 per cent) more flavour and will give more pleasure.

Chocolate and orange go extremely well together. One Easter, while in France with my daughter and two young friends from Britain, we had Sunday lunch in a good restaurant in Normandy. My pleasure came from looking at their faces during the meal, served by attentive waiters. For pudding one child chose chocolate mousse: an individual mousse, with a light vanilla custard all round, perfectly topped with a slice of orange cooked in syrup—simple, with a distinctive touch.

MOUSSE AU CHOCOLAT
Chocolate Mousse

For 6 people
200 g/7 oz good, dark chocolate,
2 tbsp water
80 g/3 oz butter
3 eggs
1 small glass of Cointreau (or 1 tbsp orange flower water)
60 g/2 oz caster sugar.
1 orange

Separate the eggs. Melt the chocolate slowly with the water. Add the butter, beaten egg yolks, Cointreau and sugar. Whisk the egg whites until they are stiff. Add one spoonful of whisked egg whites to the chocolate mixture, then add the rest of the

168

whites; with a lifting movement, mix gently and fill individual moulds or ramekins. Decorate with orange slices cooked in syrup.

PRUNEAUX AU VIN
Prunes with Wine

One lunch time, years ago, I served prune mousse with port, *mousse de pruneaux au porto*. My guest enjoyed it. 'It reminded me of the nursery' he said as an afterthought, with a smile. Was he being complimentary or had I made a *faux-pas* in serving prunes for lunch? Prunes in Britain are thought of as a *necessity*, not as an enjoyable pudding, whatever the guise. Prunes cooked in red wine and flavoured with orange are colourful, easily prepared and very pleasant. They are equally good cooked in white wine flavoured with cinnamon.

For 6 to 8 people
½ kg/1 lb medium sized soft prunes
½ litre/17½ fl. oz red wine
2 medium sized oranges with thick skin
1 cinnamon stick, broken into 2—3 pieces
50 g/2 oz sugar or more to taste
200 g/7 oz glacé orange peel, cut into strips or thin strips of
    peel of 2 oranges (removed with a potato peeler)

Soak the prunes for a couple of hours, remove the stones, cover and cook gently for 30 minutes in wine with the glacé peel (or orange peel) and cinnamon. The wine becomes darker and turns syrupy as it cooks and evaporates. Cool and serve very cold, arranged in a dish with or without cream; good vanilla ice-cream or brown bread ice-cream combines well with the prunes. Two styles of old fashioned cooking, French and British, in a good *entente cordiale*.

If some prunes are left over, purée them, add two egg yolks, three whisked egg whites and turn into a hot soufflé. Delicious with a *crème anglaise* flavoured with armagnac, brandy, malt whisky or simple crushed praline. 169

SABLÉS
Fine Orange Shortbreads

Finally, here is a recipe for sophisticated little biscuits (a French version of thin shortbread). They are delicately flavoured with orange and give the finishing touch to light, fruity or creamy puddings. They are best eaten fresh but can be kept in an airtight tin.

For 20 biscuits
250 g/½ lb flour
175g/6 oz soft butter
150 g/5 oz caster sugar
1 egg yolk
Finely grated rind of 2 oranges

Mix all the ingredients together quickly. Roll them out as thin as possible and cut out little rounds or triangles. Place them carefully on a baking tray and bake in a hot oven (200C/400F/ mark 6) for about 15 minutes or until they are just beginning to colour. Cool on a wire tray.

A more traditional way of making this biscuit is to rub the peel with sugar lumps to extract the aromatic essence instead of adding the grated rind and the sugar separately.

Desserts
de Grand-mère

DESSERTS DE GRAND-MÈRE
Granny's Puddings

The nursery puddings of old England have not quite the equivalent in France. Granny's puddings, *les desserts de grand-mere*, were made for all, and enjoyed by all, *en famille*. The fashion changes, the *pâtissier* produces more and more enticing cakes, especially at weekends, but many old fashioned puddings live on. They seem to taste better on Sundays when family and friends gather together to celebrate a birthday, a special Saint's day or merely because of tradition. There is brisk business at the florist's on Sunday mornings—flowers for the hostess, mother, grandmother, aunt or friend. The assistant is kept busy arranging bouquets, it is part of the service.

To me the old fashioned pudding *par excellence* is Snow Eggs, *Oeufs à la Neige*, or its variation, a Floating Island. It is a light and delicate combination, made with fresh eggs, sugar, milk and vanilla pod. What looks like a simple list, with a little care and good ingredients becomes a special pudding—attractive and delicious. I believe a pudding of similar composition made in Poland is known as *sweet nothing*!

The *crème anglaise*, cool and aromatic, fills a dainty dish; on it lies a flotilla of soft meringue eggs. Colourful trickles of caramel, a sprinkling of toasted almond slivers add the finishing touch and a light crunch. Freshly baked light biscuits, *petits fours*, give a note of distinction. For such efforts, home cooking deserves a rosette or a compliment. PETITS FOURS

In France delicate *petits fours* are bought, crisp and fresh, in good *pâtisseries*—at a price, because they are hand-made and their peak is short-lived. I make them myself when the mood suits. Otherwise, bought puff pastry, with two extra turns, and sprinklings of vanilla sugar, makes crunchy and tasty *palmiers* or *sacristains*. They must be small and I like them slightly caramelised. *Langues de chat*, out of a packet, become crisper and better after a short spell in the oven. Try one end dipped in good quality melted chocolate! PALMIERS

LANGUES DE CHAT

173

GENERALITIES ABOUT EGG CUSTARD

It is more unusual in France to have a pudding served with a jug of cream (less so in Normandy probably). If a sauce is required it will more likely be an egg custard with a choice of flavouring, to personalise a pudding, contrast or accentuate a flavour. It could be vanilla, coffee, chocolate, lemon, orange, Kirsch, Cointreau, tangerine, fresh ginger, caramel etc. Another alternative is, of course, a fruit sauce, for ice-cream, sorbets, bavaroises, pancakes etc. This is called a *coulis*: the old Scottish word for it is a *cullis*.

CRÈME ANGLAISE
Egg Custard

Egg custard is simple to make, even for a novice, as long as you use very fresh eggs and follow the recipe, particularly during the last minutes.

For 6 to 8 people
A generous ½ litre/1 pint milk
1 vanilla pod
5 egg yolks—4 for a lighter custard
2—3 tbsp caster sugar (depending on taste)   303

Slit the vanilla pod in the middle, scrape as much of the inside as possible, add to the milk and bring to the boil; let it infuse for 5 minutes or so off the heat, with a lid on. The tiny dark specks inside the pod give extra flavour and a distinct appearance to the custard. For a less expensive or less special custard use the pod whole, afterwards it can be wiped and kept in a jar, ready for further use. (Thrifty grandmothers did it).

Whisk the yolks with the caster sugar until pale and fluffy; Add the hot milk a little at a time to start with. Pour the mixture back into the pan and cook on a very low heat. A *bain-marie* (double boiler) may be best for anxious beginners, or alternatively, add a rounded teaspoon of arrowroot or cornflour to the mixture. It will prevent the eggs from curdling if the temperature is too high, but be vigilant nevertheless. After a first success the confidence is gained for ever.

174   Keep stirring; the custard is ready when it coats the back

of the spoon. By then all the foam will have gone from the surface; it takes a few minutes. Cool the custard quickly. I usually
dip the bottom of the pan in cold water, stirring while it cools,
to prevent a skin forming. Sieve the custard to make it perfectly
smooth and delicate.

OEUFS À LA NEIGE
Snow Eggs

4 egg whites
2 tbsp caster sugar
Pinch of salt or squeeze of lemon juice
Caramel
Toasted almond slivers

Whisk the whites as for a usual meringue, adding a pinch of
salt or a little lemon juice. When the mixture is thick, fold in
the sugar carefully. Have ready a pan filled with hot water (not
boiling), poach dessertspoonfuls of the meringue in the hot
water, dropping the mixture into the water by rapping the spoon
briskly against the sides of the pan. Dip the spoon in cold water
before the next one. Poach 3 or 4 spoonfuls at a time, one minute
or so on each side, until firm. Remove with a slotted spoon,
and drain on absorbent paper.

PUTTING THE PUDDING TOGETHER:

When the meringue and the custard are cool, float the eggs in
the custard, piling them towards the centre. Shortly before serving make the caramel with sugar and water (100 g/4 oz sugar
and 2 tbsp water). Run it over the meringue in a decorative
fashion, sprinkle the toasted almonds and then enjoy this old
fashioned, light pudding.

There can be an infinity of variations, the imagination takes
over, the season gives its seal. Instead of flavouring the custard
with vanilla use Kirsch, Cointreau or good coffee. The
meringue in turn could be flavoured with ground almond (75g/
3 oz) or a little crushed praline (2 tbsp)—pink praline for a
special romantic occasion. These things make cooking fun.

For a Cointreau custard, flavour the soft meringues with a
sprinkling of wafer-thin strips of glacé orange (either bought

or home-made). A buttery and sharp orange sauce with Cointreau added before serving would make a special fruity creation: orange juice thickened with cornflour and, off the heat, a little butter whisked in. With a coffee custard decorate the snow eggs with a thick chocolate sauce instead of caramel.

For a light interpretation and less calories, at the height of the season purée 2 lbs of ripe strawberries to replace the egg custard, add very little sugar to the fruit, as the meringues are already sweet. Lemon juice added to the puree heightens the flavour. A mixture of pureed soft berries offers a more sophisticated flavour.

ÎLE FLOTTANTE
A Floating Island

Make the egg custard then prepare the meringue with the whites of 4 eggs as in the previous recipe. This will make an island. Make a caramel with 100 g/4 oz sugar and 2 tablespoons water and coat a deep mould with it. Spoon the meringue into the mould and put in a *bain-marie*. Bake in a warm oven (175C/355F/ mark 4) for about 30 minutes, or until set, then cool. The meringue will be firm but soft to the touch. Dip the mould in hot water for a few seconds to melt the caramel, then turn into a shallow bowl. Pour the custard all around it, and there is your floating island. Sprinkle with home-made crushed praline or a few toasted, slivered almonds. Alternatively, puréed apple, flavoured with a little Calvados or pear brandy, or warmed apricot jam and a little Kirsch or Amaretto, will make unusual accompaniments.

CRÈME ANGLAISE AU VIN
Wine Custard

For a change, turn a baked custard into a wine custard. Substitute the wine for the milk and flavour with light honey and a little cinnamon stick. An adventurous approach it seems, but in fact it is a very old recipe, born in a land of vineyards.

For 6 to 8 people

4—6 egg yolks

½ litre/17½ oz sweet wine
Grated rind of lemon
100 g/4 oz light honey or sugar
Cinnamon stick (small)
Caramel — 100 g sugar / 2 tbsp water

Coat a pyrex dish with the caramel. As the wine is heating, infuse for a few minutes with the cinnamon stick and flavour with honey. Beat the yolks, add the lemon rind and mix with the wine and then proceed as with egg custard. Pour into the caramel coated dish. Put it in a *bain-marie* and bake in the oven (180C/370F/mark 4) for about half an hour. When set, turn on to a decorative plate and serve cold.

POMMES EN GELÉE
Apple Aspic

Among granny's puddings another favourite is apple aspic, or apple jelly. It is easy, looks good, tastes good and is not expensive, but it is a little lengthy; apples to peel and gentle cooking to watch. On the other hand it can be prepared in advance and kept in the fridge, covered, for up to one week, a great bonus for any cook. Use eating apples, mixing varieties maybe.

For 6 to 8 people
1 kg/2 lbs eating apples (keep the peel and cores)
¼ litre/9 fl.oz water
A good ¼ litre cider
Grated peel of 1 lemon
½ tsp pure vanilla extract
350 g/12 oz sugar

Wash, peel, core and cut the apples into thick slices. To make a really effective jelly, boil the peel, pips and cores in the water for 15 to 20 minutes. Sieve the liquid then add the grated lemon peel and the vanilla extract. Make up to half a litre with the cider and bring to the boil. Stir in the sugar then add the sliced apples and, with the lid on to start with, cook gently for about an hour. The juice will thicken, the apples will turn golden and translucent. From then on, watch very closely and keep stirring, since the pudding might turn rapidly into a brown caramel and 177 frustration would be great. Take off the heat and cool. When lukewarm, turn into a mould that has been rinsed but not dried, it will be easier to turn the pudding onto a serving dish later. Keep overnight in the fridge. Rinse the serving dish and the jellied apples will slide into position without problem. In the autumn add one sliced quince, it brings a lovely and unusual flavour plus an even firmer texture.

This pudding can be served with or without poached fruit (apples are best) and with a variety of sauces. The easiest is a jug of light cream or a bowl of unsweetened sour cream as a contrast, or simply yoghurt, flavoured with vanilla, never vanilline which is artificial.

Naturally a light egg custard, cool and fragrant with vanilla or Calvados or pear brandy is very suitable. Before serving, whisk two whites of eggs into the egg custard—it becomes light, airy and elegant. The whisked whites added when the custard is hot do keep, whereas whites added to the cold custard liquify after a while.

POMMES EN NEIGE
Apple Snow

An old fashioned nanny assured me once that all children liked Apple Snow. The pleasant fruitiness and the light texture make it an ideal nursery pudding. It is a simple pudding: well flavoured thick apple purée, whisked white of egg, with yolk for extra nourishment or a little cream. It is always eaten to the last spoonful.

This retired nanny came to my rescue for a month or so; she was full of fascinating stories from the past. Once with her charges she stayed at the Ritz for a long spell. The food was so good that she looked permanently pregnant. Halfway through her stay with me, having sampled many of our meals *en famille*, she told me that she was eating so well it was like going to a dinner party every night. A compliment I treasured— making people happy is a cook's reward. Maybe in the early days she sampled this older version of Apple Snow, without egg whites; a lengthy affair then. The use of electric whisks brings it once again into the pudding repertoire.

For 6 people
1 kg/2 lb good eating apples (Cox's orange pippin, for example)
1 small quince or lemon peel for flavour
100 g/4oz sugar
1 sachet gelatine (or 6 leaves)
2 tbsp water

Wash the apples and quince well and cut into quarters, peel and core and add the sugar and water. Cook in a hot oven for 25 to 30 minutes, with the lid on until soft. Purée the fruit; the old-fashioned *mouli-légumes* is best because it purées and sieves at the same time. Melt the gelatine in a little water, (I keep it in a *bain-marie* until dissolved) add to the warm purée. When it is cool and beginning to set start beating the mixture in a deep bowl with an electric whisk. It takes 10 to 15 minutes. The mixture thickens and becomes more and more fluffy and voluminous. When it is very thick and white fill a mould rinsed first with water. Keep in a cool place for 4 hours. Last time I made it for Valentine's Day, in a heart-shaped mould, it looked exquisite. Serve with a red light fruit purée for contrast. Apricot sauce with orange teams up well too.

OMELETTE SUCRÉE AUX POMMES
Sweet Omelette with Apple

Sweet omelettes are quick to prepare and the answer to a crisis in the kitchen when a pudding is needed without delay. There is a great choice of fillings according to what is at hand. The *omelette sucrée* can be simply nice and tasty, or sophisticated and delicate. The easiest filling is good jam, with or without a liqueur. Alternatives are orange marmalade and a spoonful of whisky or Kirsch, or apricot jam with a couple of crushed amarettis. This is a classic recipe.

For 4 people
½ kg/1 lb good eating apples
6 eggs (or 8, according to appetite)
1 large glass cider (or wine or apple juice)
Lemon peel (or cinnamon)
50 g/2 oz butter (or butter and oil)
2 lots of 50 g/2 oz caster sugar
A little oil

Cook the apples in the cider with the thin lemon peel, or cinnamon and 2 oz of sugar. When the liquid is well reduced and
syrupy take off the heat. Remove the cinnamon or lemon peel.
(Alternatively the lemon peel can be chopped finely and left in
the apples). Use a non-stick frying pan to cook the omelette—it
needs less fat and the whole process is easier. Whisk the eggs
together with the second lot of sugar, add to the pan when the
fat is hot, but not too hot. As the eggs begin to set, reduce the
heat, lift a corner of the omelette to let more liquid go under-
neath and repeat this; then draw the omelette towards you
(while it is still cooking) with a wooden spoon. It gives a lovely
pleated effect. When the omelette is almost cooked and still
creamy, arrange the warm fruit in its centre and fold it over.
Carefully slide into a warm buttered dish. Several possibilities
follow:

Serve the omelette as it is, sprinkled with caster sugar or add
a glass of warm calvados (or brandy, rum or whisky) and set
alight. Alternatively sprinkle with caster sugar and caramelise
quickly under a hot grill. With icing sugar and a hot poker, give
an attractive criss-cross finish to the dish. With time in hand,
a border of sliced apples fried in a little butter and sugar (with
cinnamon to taste) makes the omelette even more tasty and
substantial.

MERVEILLES
Wonder Pastries

Two women carrying triumphantly a large basket lined with
white napkins, filled with merveilles (golden puff pastries): it
is a memory of early childhood, at harvest, when machines
needed lots of men, many of whom came to help from
neighbouring farms. They worked hard, they ate superbly.
Each cook wanted to do best, and, if merveilles were her speciality, it was a good showpiece at the end of the meal and a favourite
one at the end of the day—the sweet touch that softens a tired
mind or body.

Merveilles are linked with fun and gatherings. This type of
180 fried pastry, lighter than fritters, is found all over the south of

France, spilling over the other side of the Pyrenees into Spain and beyond.

A friend tells me that he remembers a similar pastry in his native Poland. It is a very old recipe, suitable for any setting; teenage parties (they are enthusiastic guests), picnics, dinner parties. Served with a sprinkling of icing sugar, a bowl of red-currant *coulis* (or fruit sauce), they acquire a sophisticated touch that suits them well.

Merveilles are easy, versatile, fun to make, even a hundred at a time. They are best eaten on the same day, but sprinkled with sugar they keep reasonably well in an airtight tin. Over the years I have tried several recipes. This is my favourite one, very similar to my mother's. It is easy to double or treble the ingredients for any number of people you require.

For 10 people
300 g/10 oz sifted flour
1 level tsp baking powder (optional)l).
80 g/3 oz butter
3 large eggs
½ tsp salt
1 tbsp sugar
Rind of 1 lemon, finely grated
Rind of 1 orange, finely grated
3 spoonfuls of orange blossom water (or rum or malt whisky)
1 litre/2 pints oil for frying
100 g/4 oz icing sugar

Mix the flour, baking powder, butter, eggs, salt, sugar, rinds and liquid very thoroughly in a bowl; the dough should be firm and no longer sticky. Cover and rest for 4—5 hours minimum in a warm place. Roll out the dough as thinly as possible (3 or 4 millimetres) using only a little ball of dough at a time. It is easier if you sprinkle the rolling pin with a little flour. A noodle making machine would give the ideal thickness without effort for great quantities. According to your preference, cut the pastry into triangles, strips, crescents, but once started keep to the same shape, it looks better. Fry in oil using a large frying pan—two good inches of oil (5—6 cm) are quite enough, add more as required. The oil must be moderately hot. Cook 4 to 5 pastries at a time, according to the size of the pan. Each batch takes

2 or 3 minutes. Seconds after they are in the pan they begin to swell, balloon and float upwards; turn over and cook until golden. Remove with a slotted spoon onto absorbent paper and sprinkle with icing sugar whilst hot. They are delicious, easy to make and surprisingly light.

In the past, in my part of the world, traditionally they were fried in goose fat; I do prefer oil, besides it is easier to buy! For *la Chandeleur*, on 2nd February, everybody made merveilles and many still do. Recently, during a stay in France, a young friend asked us to tea. To my surprise and delight, we enjoyed *a nice cup of tea* with merveilles. Tea, *à la française*—a definite sign that cooking is alive, adapts and adopts.

GÂTEAU DE MA TANTE
Aunty's Apple Cake

This recipe comes from a Breton *au pair* girl, who got it from her aunt and always referred to it as *Le gâteau de ma tante*—Aunty's cake. This apple pudding is easy to make. It is fruity and tasty, and not too rich.

For 5 to 6 people
7 rounded dsp flour
4 dsp oil
3 eggs
750 g/1½ lb sliced and peeled eating apples
4 dsp sugar
2 dsp Calvados (or brandy or malt whisky)

Mix all the ingredients together, stir in the apples and pour into a well-buttered flan dish. Cook in a moderately hot oven (200c/390F/mark 6) for 20 minutes. At this point take the pudding out of the oven (using thick gloves!) and spread with the following mixture:
2 yolks
75 g/3 oz soft unsalted butter
2 dsp brown sugar
Mix these ingredients together and spread over the top of the apples. Finish cooking for another 15 minutes, or until nicely coloured. Eat warm, the flavour is better. Occasionally I replace the butter by the same quantity of cream.

TARTE ALSACIENNE
Alsatian Tart

This is a light, fruity apple tart, more sophisticated than the previous recipes and, again, prepared in two instalments.

For 5 to 6 people
1 kg/2 lb good eating apples peeled and cored, each apple cut into 8 pieces
75 g/3 oz unsalted butter
100 g/4 oz white or light brown sugar.

Second stage:
3 eggs
50 g/2 oz flour
½ litre/1 pint creamy milk
50 g/2 oz sugar

Peel and core the apples and cut each one into 8 pieces. Cook them with the butter. When they begin to soften and colour add the sugar. The spicy flavour of brown sugar goes well with apples. Reduce the heat and cook until lightly caramelised. Do not stir too much. The quantity of sugar can be reduced to taste. Straightaway spread the apples in a shallow baking dish (30 cm/ 12 ins in diameter) and pour over it the mixture made with the eggs, creamy milk, flour and 2 oz of sugar. Bake in a warm oven (190C/375F/mark 5) until golden—around 25 minutes.

Serve warm, on its own or with a light vanilla or lemony egg custard. It makes a good contrast of flavour and texture.

CLAFOUTIS
Cherry Pudding

Traditionally, this French pudding is made with black cherries. Change the name and the flavour by using pears, plums, grapes or apples.

In my chapter on pancakes I mention thick pancakes made with stoned cherries. This was the ancestor of the *Clafoutis*, made when ovens were less common or predictable. It is fun to follow progress through the kitchen.

This is light, simple country fare, easy to make, extremely 183 tasty and attractive. Double the quantities (increase the cooking time) and feed plenty without fuss.

For 4 to 5 people
A good ½ kg/1 lb black cherries
⅓ litre/12 fl. oz creamy milk
3 tbsp flour
3 tbsp caster sugar (the quantity varies according to the sweetness of the fruit and personal taste)
3 eggs and 1 yolk
A few drops of almond extract or 2 tbsp Kirsch
Butter to grease round a shallow tin

To make the batter whisk the eggs and sugar together. Mix in the flour and milk a little at a time. Butter the dish, arrange the stoned cherries to cover the base completely (traditionally the stones were left in to improve the flavour, a drop of almond extract or some Kirsch could be used to that effect). Cover the cherries with the batter. Cook in a medium to hot oven for 30 to 40 minute (the centre must be firm). Sprinkle with icing sugar and eat warm.

FLOGNARDE AUX POIRES
Pears in Batter

For 4 to 5 people
500—600 g/1 lb of pears
100 g/3½ oz flour
4 eggs
100 g/3½ oz sugar
¾ litre/1¼ pint milk
1 small glass Calvados or Armagnac

Peel and slice the pears, arrange them evenly like a star in a well-buttered oven dish or gratin dish. Pour the batter over the fruit. Cook like the *cherry clafoutis*, but in a hotter oven this time, to get a puffed effect. Serve warm preferably, with a cool light egg custard, flavoured with a vanilla pod (cut open, and with as much of the insides as possible scraped into the milk). The custard with its myriad of tiny black specks is very aromatic and delectable.

184   For a change, good eating apples and pears could be mixed.

Alternatively, prunes soaked in strong tea or water mixed with a little brandy, or malt whisky, are delicious, the effect most attractive. Sprinkle with icing sugar before serving.

DESSERT AUX PRUNES
Plum Pudding

The first time I tried apple pudding made with puréed apples, breadcrumbs and cream, I enjoyed the pleasant flavour and smooth texture. All the same, it lacked sharpness and character. With the flavour of Victoria plums, sharp and distinctive, rough breadcrumbs caramelised with butter and sugar, the taste of this pudding is quite different: a contrast of crunchy and smooth textures, sharp and sweet flavours.

For 4 to 6 people
700 g/1½ lb plums (stoned)
150 g/5 oz sugar
150 g/5 oz stale bread
50 g/2 oz butter
200 ml/6 fl.oz whipping cream (or mixture of smooth yoghurt with cream)

Cook the stoned plums with very little water and just over half of the sugar, to taste; put aside to cool. Rub the bread between the fingers to make coarse breadcrumbs and fry gently in the butter. When they become crisp and coloured add the rest of the sugar and caramelise the breadcrumbs stirring until cool to avoid lumps or dark caramel.

Fill a pretty looking bowl with the cold stewed plums (if there is too much liquid I add a little cornflour as soon as they finish stewing). Add the layer of breadcrumbs (not too early before the meal to avoid sogginess). Smooth the cream (or cream and yoghurt mix) evenly over the top of the breadcrumbs.

Gooseberries can be used in this recipe with equal success.

GLACE AU PAIN BIS
Brown Bread Ice-Cream

This is made the easy way with bought, good quality ice-cream. Traditionally, ice-cream is made with *crème anglaise* enriched

with cream, flavoured with vanilla, coffee, chocolate, rum or
praline.

Brown bread ice-cream, an old English recipe, tastes rather
like a praline ice-cream. This version is quick and good.

75 g/3 oz brown bread crumbs
1 dsp brown sugar
1 litre/1¾ pints good quality ice-cream

Bake the breadcrumbs until crisp then sprinkle with sugar to
caramelise them slightly. Stir once or twice to make sure they
are evenly caramelised. While cooling, keep stirring to avoid
the formation of lumps. When cold, stir into the softened ice-
cream. Put back into the deep-freeze (or freezing compartment
of the refrigerator). It is excellent served with a cold, smooth
apricot sauce (or hot for contrast) or with puréed prunes
flavoured with cinnamon.

PÂTE À CHOUX
Chou Pastry

This is much easier to make than people fear, provided the
recipe is followed carefully. It soon becomes *un jeu d'enfants*—
child's play, or nearly so! It is good, versatile and elegant, and
can be sweet or savoury.

250 ml/8 fl. oz water
1 tsp sugar (omitted for savoury choux)
Salt—a generous pinch (none if salted butter is used)
80 g/3 oz butter
125 g/4½ oz flour
4 medium-sized eggs

Pour the water into a pan, add the butter cut into pieces, the
salt or sugar, and bring to the boil. At this point the butter
should be completely melted, and the mixture frothy and rising
to the top. Add all the flour, take the pan off the heat and mix
briskly with a wooden spoon. Replace on the heat (a gentle heat)
stirring until the mixture comes away from the pan, forming
into a glossy ball. It takes 2 or 3 minutes to dry the mixture.
Take the pan off the heat and keep stirring for a few minutes
186 to cool the mixture. Now add the first egg. It is essential to

mix each egg thoroughly with the mixture before adding the next one. Once the mixture looks smooth again and the egg has been completely absorbed proceed with the next one. According to the quantity of flour and the size of the eggs, the fourth egg may not be required entirely. Beat it up, as for an omelette, and add to the mixture a little at a time. The pastry must be neither thick nor runny. When lifted up with a spoon it falls down like a ribbon.

For a small chou, a walnut-sized piece of pastry is required; for a larger one a piece the size of a very small egg will do. Arrange the pastry on a baking tray, leaving space for growth between them, like a gardener planting a patch of cabbages *en quinconce* (staggered). A pastry bag helps to make perfect and even choux. Otherwise use two teaspoons dipped in hot water, one to take the amount required and the other to ease it off onto the baking tray. According to the size of the chou, the cooking time is 25 to 30 minutes. Cook in a hot oven (210C/420F/mark 6). Whatever the temptation do not open the door for at least 15 minutes. If after the first 20 minutes, the choux appear to colour too quickly lower the temperature. When the choux are ready, turn off the heat and leave in the oven with the door ajar. They must be light and hollow inside, firm but not too crisp outside.

The sooner the choux are eaten the better, unless they are cooled and kept in the deep-freeze for later use. They can be freshened up in a warm oven when required. Once filled, the choux must be eaten within a day. A teaspoon of this pastry deep fried turns into a 'wind puff'. Sprinkle with icing sugar and eat warm.

Tiny choux pastries, *profiteroles*, are traditionally filled with vanilla ice cream, or cream, and served with hot chocolate sauce. Choux buns (*choux à la crème*) and èclairs are filled with pastry cream flavoured with Kirsch, chocolate, coffee etc. The pastry cream, while still warm, can be enriched with a little thick cream or butter stirred into it.

A chou bun filled with a savoury mixture becomes a *caroline*. Fill with a mixture of vegetables cut into small cubes with mayonnaise and mustard, for example, or chicken and tarragon mayonnaise or with fish and mushrooms.

A large ring cut in half horizontally and filled with coffee butter-cream is a *Paris-Brest*. A Parisian *pâtissier* wanting to

celebrate the Paris to Brest cycle race created the cake in the shape of a wheel. A large chou bun crowned with a smaller one

and bound together with chantilly is a *religieuse*, a nun!

A *St Honoré* is made with a round short-crust pastry base with a border of chou pastry supporting a garland of choux buns bound with caramel. St Honoré is the patron saint of pastry-cooks and bakers! The inside of the *St Honoré* is filled with pastry cream enriched with cream (to taste) and bound with gelatine. It is a very festive pudding which lives up to its looks — light and tasty.

French christenings, weddings and especially first com-

munions would not be the same without a *pièce montée*, a pyramid of choux buns, filled with Kirsch or vanilla flavoured pastry cream, and stuck together with a caramel. It takes a lot of experience and *savoir faire* to reach perfection in the making of this culinary scaffolding. I know it well, I worked late into the night with a friend from Paris making my wedding cake. The local baker, who may have been disappointed not to be asked to provide the traditional fruit cake, made sure that I had the right cake for our son's christening and delivered one with his compliments. Naturally it is impossible to send a piece of the *pièce montée* to absent friends. Instead, one sends white sugared almonds. For a christening, sugared almonds are blue or pink (a boy or a girl).

Finally, for a special savoury chou, add to the basic recipe 125 g/4½ oz of grated Gruyère cheese, a sprinkling of nutmeg and cayenne pepper. Cook them like choux buns and eat warm with a drink before dinner or as a starter.

GÂTEAU AU YAOURT
Yoghurt Cake

Yoghurts have been popular in France for a very long time. Their mild, velvety flavour soon made them top of the list for simple puddings. The natural fruit flavours and colours increased their popularity further.

The following recipe is a child's recipe, or just about, because

they like baking cakes and because this one is done the easy

way. No weighing is required—a great incentive for young children. Simply use a carton of plain yoghurt. This will then be
used as a measure for the other ingredients.

1 carton plain yoghurt
3 cartons self-raising flour (or plain flour with 2 level tsp baking
  powder)
1 carton sugar ($1\frac{1}{2}$ cartons for a sweet tooth)
$\frac{3}{4}$ carton plain oil
4 eggs
Juice and grated rind of a lemon or orange
1 oz of butter for the baking tin

Mix all the ingredients together. (For a lighter cake separate
the whites of eggs and whisk until stiff, with a little salt or a
few drops of lemon. Add to the mixture gently and with a lifting
movement.) Fill a well greased baking cake dish. Bake in a warm
oven (180C/350F/mark 4) for a full 45 minutes. Check that the
cake is cooked, leave in the oven for a few minutes with the
door ajar.

The flavour can be changed by adding a couple of spoonfuls
of good, dark, orange marmalade, 2 to 3 sliced apples or pears,
a little light honey (use less sugar)or ground cinnamon.

GÂTEAU AU CHOCOLAT
Chocolate Cake

Make sure the chocolate is good, the extra expense is well worth
it. Not long ago, when I was looking for a good baking chocolate,
the shopkeeper pointed out a block of inexpensive chocolate and
said, 'What about this—science nowadays can do anything.' I
said nothing!

A few years ago, wherever we went in France, we were offered
gâteau au chocolat de grand-mère et sa crème anglaise. It is one
of these old-fashioned recipes, well proven and timeless, that
reappear now and then; slightly changed maybe, but always
popular, irresistible to chocolate lovers. It is a straightforward
recipe. One can always change the flavour and aroma by adding
coffee, alcohol, orange or ginger.

200 g/7 oz black or bitter chocolate
4 eggs and 1 white

50 g/2 oz plain flour or ground almonds
100 g/4 oz butter
100 g/4 oz caster sugar

Melt very slowly the chocolate with the butter, add the yolks and the flour, then carefully mix in the stiffly beaten egg whites (as for a meringue). Generously butter a cake tin and pour in the mixture. Bake in a warm oven (180c/350F/mark 4) for 45 minutes or so. The cooking must be slow. Leave in the oven for a few extra minutes with the door open. Properly cooked, the centre should be soft, the cake heavy. It is not supposed to be a light sponge. Sprinkle with icing sugar, and if you feel like it, when it is cold, add a delicate note using a stencil: a star, or a heart or any design that suits you.

The cake is so rich that small portions are *de rigueur*. Serve with a light, cool *crème anglaise* which can be flavoured with coffee. The contrast is perfect.

To finish this last section, here are some little extravagances which bring back the tastes of summer fruits on winter nights. They make splendid presents but that is the subject for another book. Here are a few meanwhile.

When the cherries are ripe again, it is time to fill jars with fruit and brandy, or vodka. In the south they were pickled in plain *eau de vie*, strong and fiery. A syrup is more necessary than ever in this case. My father did not agree with that—the stronger the better, he said! Because there were plenty of cherries and cheap *eau de vie*, the jars were large, and brought out whenever a visitor came along. It is nice to know that these customs have not disappeared. A few of these cherries can be used to flavour puddings, fruit salads and cakes such as Black Forest Gâteau. Remember to remove the stones.

Leave a little stem on each cherry. The stones, after a few months in the alcohol, impart a delicate flavour. Fruit kept in such a high concentration of alcohol keeps for months. Enjoy these treats after dinner, in winter. Many summer fruits can be treated the same way. One of my favourites is plums in Armagnac.

In France a special *eau de vie* is used for bottling fruit. It can be bought in summer from greengrocers and supermarkets.

Just like vodka, it is tasteless and flavoured by the fruit. Cognac, Armagnac, rum and malt whisky are more expensive, but the result is especially delicious, no need to use vintage! The alcohol develops a fruity flavour and aroma—a delicious blending. *Eau de vie* is not easy to buy outside France. In general I have suggested vodka as the alternative.

Always use air-tight jars. Air getting in would spell disaster, the flavour and the aroma becoming stale. It happened to me once when using a jar sealed with a large cork that seemed to be adequate. Kilner jars or screw-top jars with rubber washers, are the safest bet.

REINES-CLAUDES À LA VODKA
Greengages in Vodka

1 kg/2 lb screw-top jar
1 kg/2 lb greengages, ripe and without blemishes.
225 g/$\frac{1}{2}$ lb sugar
$\frac{1}{2}$ vanilla pod
2 tbsp water
$\frac{1}{2}$ litre/17 fl.oz vodka, or enough to cover the fruit

First prick the greengages near the stem with a fine knitting needle and cut a little off the stem. Dip for a few seconds in boiling water, drain and fill the jar. At this point, add the alcohol to the syrup (made with sugar and a little water). Half a vanilla pod infused in the syrup gives a delicious aroma, especially when using plain vodka. Pour over the fruit. Marinate for 3 to 4 months.

CONFITURE DU CÉLIBATAIRE
Batchelor's Jam

The recipe will explain the name. It is easy and absolutely delectable. It is not a jam really but a mixture of fruit kept in alcohol (brandy or vodka for example) and sugar. The proportion of alcohol to sugar is 1 litre/35 fl. oz of alcohol to $\frac{3}{4}$ kg/1lb 10 oz sugar, maximum. As the year progresses , fill a large jar with fruit in season, add sugar and vodka every time a new layer is added. Start with strawberries; later on a few wild ones bring a wonderful aroma. Cherries, cutting off a little of the stems, large dessert gooseberries (sweeter and larger than the ordinary variety), a few raspberries, medium-sized ripe greengages, apricots, peaches cut into quarters (the almond inside the kernel adds extra flavour), a few large blackcurrants for colour and flavour, pears cut in quarters. The 'jam' must be well covered by the alcoholised syrup, the lid very tight.

Try this delicious medley around Christmas time; it should be perfect. The blend of the different fruit with the alcohol is wonderful and aromatic. Serve after dinner instead of a liqueur, or with a pudding.

LIQUEUR DE CASSIS
Cassis Liqueur

Blackcurrant liqueur was traditionally made at home. Recipes vary a little, the result is always rewarding: fruity, aromatic and with a deep colour. It is delicious on its own, with sorbets or red fruit salad. Occasionally, and quite successfully, I have made a version of Black Forest Gâteau, replacing the cherries by blackcurrants flavoured with the liqueur. Nothing to be compared with the black cherry version but it makes a good cake in its own right when there are plenty of blackcurrants.

In France, the best cassis liqueur comes from the Dijon area. White Burgundy wine with a little liqueur is a traditional aperitif called *vin blanc cassis* but better known everywhere as Kir. The Abbé Kir, once Mayor of Dijon, decided that, at functions organised by the Town Hall, *vin blanc cassis* would be the official aperitif—a clever move that sold lots of liqueur everywhere. It is a pleasant summer drink. Occasionally it is replaced by raspberry liqueur, but I still prefer the cassis flavour.

1 litre/$1\frac{3}{4}$ pints vodka
1 kg/2 lb good quality blackcurrants
$\frac{3}{4}$ kg/$1\frac{1}{2}$ lb sugar
1 dozen fresh blackcurrant leaves
1—2 cloves (optional)

In the bottom of a large jar (or two small ones) with a tight lid, lay young leaves, bruised beforehand. Add the cloves, the
192 berries, then the sugar. Pour the vodka over them and close

the jars tightly. Keep them in the sun—I keep mine on the kitchen window sill, a fortifying sight! After three months, sieve the mixture, crush the berries thoroughly, throw away the leaves and put back in the jar.

After another month, sieve the liqueur through muslin and squeeze out as much juice as possible. Let the liqueur rest for a couple of days and fill the bottles. From then on keep in a cool, dark place. Drink within the year for better flavour.

RAISINÉ
Autumn Fruit Preserve

To close the season, here is an unusual jam made with red or white grape juice. At the beginning of the *vendanges* (grape gathering) in the south of France, each family kept some *moût* (grape juice from the press) to make *raisiné*. It was most useful during and just after the war because no sugar was required; the sweetness of the grapes and lengthy cooking gave a well flavoured and dark syrup in which the autumn fruits were cooked together. Nowadays some sugar is added—it curtails the cooking time.

Press or squeeze out the juice from 3 kg/6 lbs grapes. Cook the juice for half an hour or so. At this point, when it is thicker, add 225 g/$\frac{1}{2}$ lb sugar for each litre/$\frac{3}{4}$ pint of liquid, and all the varieties of fresh fruit you can find, chopped fairly finely. Here is a choice of some fruit: cooking pears, quinces, figs, melon, peaches, slices of pumpkin, a few walnuts, apples, and even some tender carrots. Try to add these fruits to the *raisiné* early or late in the cooking according to their texture (hard fruits first). Cook gently for an hour or so. This mixture does not set very firmly. In fact it can be used more as a pudding than a jam. The flavours and textures are good. It is pleasant served with ice-cream, plain sponge or shortbread.It takes me back to early childhood and an easy life in the sun.

INDEX